PARENTING TEEN BOYS

PARENTING TEEN BOYS

A POSITIVE PARENTING APPROACH TO RAISING HEALTHY, INDEPENDENT SONS

MARISSA GARCIA SORIA, MSW, LCSW

ROCKRIDGE
PRESS

Interior and Cover Designer: Angela Navarra
Art Producer: Melissa Malinowksy
Editor: John Makowski
Production Editor: Ruth Sakata Corley
Production Manager: Lanore Coloprisco

All illustrations used under license from iStock

Paperback ISBN: 978-1-63807-992-7
eBook ISBN: 978-1-63878-513-2
R0

This book is dedicated to the cycle breakers. Know that your choices are making a change, not just for you, but for your children and generations to come.

CONTENTS

INTRODUCTION

Welcome to *Parenting Teen Boys!* I am Marissa Garcia Soria, a licensed clinical social worker, working in mental health services for the last 20 years. I obtained my master of social work in 2009, after working with South Los Angeles youth as a behavior intervention specialist. My experience with teens and their families ranges from community mental health services and medical social work to school settings and my own group practice.

Working with young children and teens sparks a passion for me to create and ignite change in teens' lives while helping them learn to healthily and effectively communicate their needs and emotions. This also allows me to engage with parents to aid them in supporting their teens in breaking away from unhealthy cycles and patterns of behaviors and interactions—increasing effective communication that leads to improved relationships! Yes, dealing with teens is tough. Grant yourself and your son some kindness and grace as you both navigate through the bumpy roads of puberty and adolescence.

This book is designed to provide you with knowledge about your teen—and your parenting techniques—to help you both get through these tough years. This book offers you support in addressing some of the difficult and sticky issues that many parents of teens face. It provides new information in a non-judgmental manner so that you can gain familiarity with some of your son's inner workings. I hope to guide you into breaking away from unhealthy parenting patterns that might be part of inter-generational or cultural dynamics and instead implement new modes of communication with your son in order to inspire him to thrive as a healthy and successful adult.

The goal is to help you gain a deeper and clearer understanding of some of the physiological and social issues that your son might experience, while also giving you the tools to aid in keeping him safe. This book will also provide positive parenting tips as a modality. As you implement these techniques in your home, communication should improve, trust will increase, and long-lasting bonds should form with your child as he becomes an adult.

Teens are a lot smarter and more aware than they are typically given credit for, so if he feels that this parenting style and its techniques are being used to control or manipulate him, he will be less likely to participate. I wish you the best in this journey, and have faith in your love and compassion for your son and your relationship. You got this!

WHAT IS POSITIVE PARENTING?

Positive parenting was introduced to the United States in the 1920s by two Viennese psychiatrists. Positive parenting is defined by best-selling author Pamela Li as "a parenting principle that assumes children are born good and with the desire to do the right thing. It emphasizes the importance of mutual respect and using positive ways to discipline. The positive parenting approaches focus on teaching proper future behavior instead of punishing past misbehavior." Positive parenting calls for firm boundaries while also allowing for mistakes, problem-solving, and meeting your son where he is in his current developmental stage. Positive parenting steers away from a punitive mindset to resolve mistakes or defiant behavior.

Positive parenting is deemed authoritative, which studies have found to be the most effective form of parenting. Some of the benefits of the implementation of this style of parenting include fewer behavioral problems, closer parent-child relationships, improved self-esteem and well-being, greater school performance, better social skills, greater self-esteem, and less stress for parents.

The transition to positive parenting can be challenging. This book will help parents navigate shifting cycles and create bonds with their teenage boys in a way that will hopefully last into adulthood. Positive parenting requires effective communication with your teen, allowing space for your teen to not feel talked at, but instead engaged in mutual conversation. Teenagers typically go through a phase of icing parents out with disrespectful attitudes, talking back, one-word answers, and the ever so cringeworthy "I don't know"—complete with a shrug for extra *oomph*!

Allow yourself to take space to identify the feelings that come up as you explore the realm of positive parenting. How were you parented? What are the takeaways you want to continue in your parenting journey with your teen? What unhealthy cycles do you hope to break? Take a moment to write those down. Now think about the conversations you were not allowed to have with your parents as you were going through puberty and finding your place in the world—as you explored your identity, self-worth, and relationships with your family and friends.

Positive parenting encourages you to engage your child in conversation while allowing him to explore his strengths, respect boundaries, and own his voice. The most significant takeaway is this: Do what you say, and say what you mean. When setting boundaries and rules, follow through with the consequences set forth. This creates structure, routine, and most important, trust.

Some key tips for the positive parenting model include the following:

1. Create awareness for yourself and your child regarding the reasons behind his behaviors and actions.

2. Be kind and firm. While parenting your son, you are also modeling problem-solving strategies for him. Keep that in mind as you speak to him.

3. Be clear and consistent. Tell him what you expect and make your conversations with him age appropriate.

4. Take breaks! Let's face it—parenting is not always easy! If things get heated, allow yourself and your son to take breaks in order to avoid falling into unhealthy conflict resolution.

Implementing positive parenting might seem like a daunting task after reading through all of this information. Remember that practice and consistency are key when transitioning to positive parenting. Positive parenting is linked to having a healthy impact on adolescent brain development, so it's worth the conscious effort.

5-STEP "EMOTION COACHING"

John Gottman, founder of the Gottman Institute, a research-based relationship initiative, developed a parenting strategy known as "emotion coaching." The philosophy behind this strategy comes from the idea that awareness of what drives emotions can decrease problematic behaviors. In essence, you will become the emotion coach for your child as he learns to identify his feelings and their connections to his actions, reactions, and behaviors. This is a five-step approach that is geared toward helping your son build emotional intelligence, self-regulation, and management of his stress responses. These are the five essential steps for emotion coaching:

1. Create awareness of your son's emotions. Recognize how and when he expresses his feelings and create that awareness for yourself and him.

2. Connect with your son. Let him know he is important and that you want to hear and learn about how he is feeling. Be open to his perspective and make a space to explore his viewpoints.

3. Listen to your son. Allow him to express his feelings and emotions, and provide an empathetic ear. Validate his feelings, letting it be known that he matters.

4. Name the emotions. Your son is learning more about emotions during this time. If you label the feelings, he will also learn how to express what he is actually feeling. Avoid telling him how he is feeling, and instead lead him in conversation in order to allow emotional exploration together. Model for him by identifying and labeling your own emotions as well.

5. Find solutions. When you identify solutions, also set limits and problem solve with him. When he misbehaves explain why you feel it was hurtful or inappropriate. Guide him in problem-solving and encourage emotional expression.

As you navigate through the chapters in this book, you will pick up new positive parenting tips. Utilize the concept of emotion coaching alongside the core beliefs of positive parenting in order to implement these tips.

HOW TO USE THIS BOOK

This book is designed to give an overview of your teen son and issues related to his adolescence. We will delve into typical teen growth and development and the impact that the people around him and other factors play on his journey into adulthood. Throughout these chapters, you will see two recurring sections: Debunking the Rumor Mill and Study Prep: Your Positive Parenting Notes. In the Debunking the Rumor Mill sections, we will address common myths and misconceptions when it comes to teen boys and address them with evidence-based research for the most accurate responses. In the Study Prep: Your Positive

Parenting Notes sections, I will offer some parenting tips based on the positive parenting model and provide you with ways in which to incorporate them in the parenting of your son.

In this book we will delve into the following topics:

- **Chapter 1: A Brief History of Teenage Boys.** The history of teen boys is discussed and includes a look at the pressures teens face in the present day. Teens desire to be unique, and this chapter reviews the struggle to belong, toxic masculinity, and common misnomers that are used when referring to boys and the negative impact those might have on your son.

- **Chapter 2: The Development of Teenage Boys.** This chapter delves into the physiological development of your son as he grows and goes through adolescence. We will discuss how testosterone plays a role in his development, and review details of the teenage brain, especially his frontal lobe, and how it impacts his behaviors and actions.

- **Chapter 3: Becoming Fluent in Teenage Boy.** Communication and how he engages with others are explored. We will gain an understanding of social media dialect for teens, the pressure of performing on social media, as well as the multiple uses he has with his social media apps. Diverse friendships, the influence of his peers, and the importance of healthy dating and what that consists of are discussed.

- **Chapter 4: The Social Lives of Teenage Boys.** Socialization is key for your teen, and his friendships during this time are a big indicator of who he is and what he is interested in. Integrating diversity and inclusivity in both his platonic friendships and intimate relationships is important at this time. Practice being supportive of his social connections—yes, even if he's hanging out with people you sorely dislike.

- **Chapter 5: Discussing Body Image & Bullying with Teenage Boys.** Body image has an impact on your son, so this chapter addresses the pressures he faces or places on himself. Learn how bullying and pressures to perform or look a certain way, especially in sports, can impact your son.

- **Chapter 6: Teaching Sex Ed to Teenage Boys.** Talking with your son about sex can be uncomfortable and awkward for him … and you. Recognize that the discomfort you both feel is normal and that the importance of having this conversation with him is key in allowing him to develop a healthy and safe sex life.

- **Chapter 7: The Self-Expression of Teenage Boys.** Your son is going through many physical changes in adolescence. He will also deliberately change his looks, including his hair and clothing, as well as his interests and friendships during this time. Remember that he is learning about who is he and what he likes as he journeys into adulthood. Allow him to have autonomy in his self-expression within limits that feel comfortable in your home, being sure to include him in the conversation.

- **Chapter 8: Talking about Drugs & Alcohol with Teenage Boys.** Drugs and alcohol are always nerve-racking topics of conversation with teens. It is essential to discuss with him the ramifications of use and misuse of drugs and alcohol as well as agreeing on a safety plan and your expectations of him.

CHAPTER 1

A BRIEF HISTORY OF TEENAGE BOYS

In this chapter, we will address the enigma that is teenage boys. Their interactions with parents and caregivers can be difficult as they are transitioning into adulthood. It sounds cliché, but hormones play a sneaky role in their social interactions and, most of all, their relationship with their parents—that's you! Understanding the thoughts and frustrations that rattle the teen brain can feel like a daunting task. Opening up to the idea of giving your teen son a voice might even feel uncomfortable and new. Challenge yourself to think of the reasons why that might be.

Together we will look at the idiosyncrasies you perhaps unknowingly engage in with your teen son. These characteristics may have been part of your cultural and societal norms for generations. Now is the time to incorporate change and break those cycles that could hinder the relationship with your teen son. Today, choose to bring about change in your parent-son dynamic, which will carry on in your continued relationship with him—and also possibly his future partner and family.

We will also navigate the history of teenage boys and some of the effects that societal, cultural, and familial expectations can have on them. The intention of this chapter is to identify and stop toxic cycles that you may not even realize you were engaging in and create effective and positive change for you and your son. We will begin to put positive parenting into practice and break down toxic masculinity and its effects on your child, family, and society. With the use of real-life examples, we will navigate through the changes you want to create with your child to improve and/or develop effective communication strategies.

AN ANTHROPOLOGICAL LOOK AT TEEN CULTURE

Teen culture took a turn in the 1960s. Racial conflict, political unrest, and the transition to desegregated schools played a huge factor in teen culture, with continued racism and aggression among different teenage groups. In Southern California, teens were impacted by racial injustice during the 1992 Los Angeles riots. According to the *Los Angeles Times*, the acquittals that sparked the riots led to feelings of anger and disillusion among teens about the world they were to inherit. In 2015, protests over the death of Freddie Gray erupted throughout social media, creating awareness of civil unrest and a space where teens could express their feelings as well as be privy to opposing views online.

Flash forward to 2020, when the world experienced a pandemic that was unprecedented in our lifetimes. Along with the unique challenges of the pandemic, our teens struggled with school pressures, family challenges, bullying, mental health issues, and hormonal changes as they developed into adulthood. Additionally, they dealt with issues related to social media, political unrest, racial injustice, and climate change, to name a few. That is a lot for any adult, much less a teen who is struggling to find their place among friends, family, and society. Although some of this probably feels similar to what you experienced as a teen, I want to challenge you to view issues through the lens of a teenage mind. What might help you feel validated and seen? What would be a good way for your voice to be heard?

Presently, male teens face many unique experiences and pressures, including but not limited to political and racial injustices, expectations of "being a man," having an acceptable number of followers on social media, pressure to produce the content necessary to feel seen and respected by their followers, and the desire to meet cultural and societal standards. During this time, your son is also trying to find his place in the world—who he is and how he wants to be perceived. The societal issues he is facing add to the intricate puzzle of your son figuring himself out.

It is important to practice empathy, patience, and kindness when approaching your teen. Recognize and aid your son in identifying some of the pressures he might feel and allow him the freedom to honestly and openly express himself. Provide a safe and nonjudgmental space where productive dialogue facilitates problem-solving and decision-making strategies. Creating this type of environment allows for your child to feel seen and heard, and leads to more effective communication so you can integrate to, rather than isolate from, your son's life.

THE STRUGGLE TO BELONG IS JUST AS REAL AS THE DESIRE TO BE UNIQUE

There are many factors that come into play for a teenager who is wavering between the need to belong and the desire to embrace their uniqueness. Some factors that might affect your son's decision-making include cultural and religious beliefs, family traditions and expectations, financial status, family unit composition, mental health, and physical health and attributes. In an era of social media, the number of *likes* tends to determine validation and self-worth. This is often a crucial part of a teen's identity, presenting a difficult dilemma for your son: being seen and validated by the amount of *likes* and followers in a social media world versus learning to socially interact in real life.

This may be a difficult concept to understand as an adult, but take a step down Memory Lane and reminisce about your teen years. What made you feel like you belonged during that stage of your life? How did it feel to *not* belong? Do you remember being comfortable with marathon phone chats but not feeling so self-confident in face-to-face encounters? Take those memories and turn them into empathy and support for your son, who has the added pressures of living in the current social media environment. Recognize the importance of not having to be "on" at all times, since social media wasn't as prevalent during your journey into adolescence.

There is an importance in creating a space where your child can take the metaphorical "mask" off. Embrace your child's uniqueness. Invite him to express his needs, emotions, and thoughts without feeling judged or put down for caring about what his friends or social media followers think of him. This is part of his journey into developing and discovering himself, so as a supportive parent, choose to be a positive part of that journey. Recognize his need to belong while also encouraging the quirks and characteristics that make him unique.

Teenage years are typically a time of discovering who we are, who we want to be, and how we want others to see us. This is when your son gets to explore his identity and develop coping skills that can be beneficial or detrimental. Self-esteem, self-worth, and self-love are significant parts of this journey. As a parent, you will have to decide whether to be a support system for your son or just another difficult aspect of your son's teenage experience. Which will you choose?

DEBUNKING THE RUMOR MILL:
ARE MODERN TEENS GROWING UP FASTER THAN THEIR PREDECESSORS?

As technology continues to move at a rapid speed, so it seems does our teens' tech savvy as well. Today's teens are exposed to technology that allows information and misinformation to flow quickly into the palm of their hands. Information, cultural dynamics, and belief systems all play huge roles in the ways teens respond to all of the issues they face. With technology and social media continuing to grow and flourish, present-day teens are privy to loads of information that wasn't so easily accessible to their predecessors. This exposes them to data that, due to developmental stages, might be difficult to process and manage as they also deal with puberty and finding a place in the community.

Teens are often pushed into maturity, expected to outperform and outsmart their counterparts through parental pressure to achieve and succeed. The line between childhood, adolescence, and adulthood becomes blurred with a backdrop of expectations, demands, and social media exposure. Technology and parental demands play a significant role in the push to "grow up."

Teenagers are often itching to be adults and engage in adult-like behaviors but do not necessarily have the emotional and cognitive capacities to handle such advanced feelings and behaviors. This can lead to regression, as well as feelings of failure and disappointment projected from parents who have placed unachievable or difficult goals on their children. This in no way means you should not have reasonable expectations of your adolescent. The goal is to create awareness and allow for the child to enter

continued >>

adolescence with guidance and nurturing that support his developmental stages and brain development.

Be cognizant of how social media plays a role in your child's pressure to perform. Ensure that you challenge your child to grow in an age-appropriate way based on his emotional and mental capacity. Then take it back to a round table with your child and have a conversation to relay the expectations you have of him, and ask him how you can best offer the support for him to meet those expectations.

FORGETTING "BOYS WILL BE BOYS" & OTHER PARENTING MISNOMERS

"Boys will be boys" has been an excuse used to justify negative and toxic behavior for years. When and how do we hold teen boys accountable for their actions? Are we perpetuating that cycle and and not even aware? What are some actions your teen boy has taken that you've justified as "boys will be boys"? Has your son made a derogatory comment about a girl's outfit or body, scoffed at chores that are assigned to him that might be considered traditionally female tasks, or perhaps exhibited outdated views on dating and curfews? Although these examples might seem minimal or insignificant, they can lead to greater discontent in family and social dynamics. Sexual assault, physical violence, and bullying are some of the behaviors that have been historically been excused by the "boys will be boys" attitude.

It is important to acknowledge that there are other parenting misnomers that contribute to a toxic mindset on your male-identifying son or his peers. Accountability time! Let's review some of the phrases listed below that may be in use and can influence toxic traits and lead to an unhealthy belief system.

Note that this is just a small sampling of the many misnomers that are used in relation with teen boys. The intention of this activity is to foster awareness that leads to change—no self-blame or shaming allowed! How many of these have you or someone you know used with a teenage boy? Although some of these may not apply, I want to challenge you to think of some other misnomers that are used in your family or culture that might also negatively affect your child, and mindfully shift those to healthy, positive statements.

1. "Stop being so sensitive."

2. "Only girls use those toys."

3. "Boys don't cry."

4. "Are you a little girl?"

5. "Winning is your only option. Don't be weak."

6. "You hit/play/throw like a girl."

7. "You want to wear *that* color?"

8. "Are you a sissy?"

9. "Why can't you be more like your brother?"

10. "It's your job to be the man of the house."

To institute change, examine these misnomers and come up with alternative statements that are more positive and less toxic. For example, instead of telling your son, "Stop being so sensitive," say to him, "Go ahead and feel what you're feeling." In doing so, you help cultivate emotional awareness for yourself, your family, and your teen son. You are providing a safe space in which your son gets to be free and belong just by being who he is.

Communicate with your son that he is loved and accepted. This requires open communication and vulnerability, as well as acceptance and willingness to implement change. This does not make you a weak parent but instead models to your child that you are capable of growth and change in all stages of life. As you begin implementing these changes into your household, I want you to think about how you will also set boundaries with others, such as teachers or grandparents, who have certain expectations or demands of your child.

WHAT PEOPLE MEAN WHEN THEY SAY "TOXIC MASCULINITY"

Toxic masculinity is a term that is used to describe behaviors that are seen as oppressive and disrespectful to women. The *Oxford English Dictionary* defines it as "a set of attitudes and ways of behaving stereotypically associated with or expected of men, regarded as having a negative impact on men and on society as a whole." There is a range of ways that toxic masculinity can infest society and your home. Some examples of toxic masculinity include but are not limited to:

- "Mansplaining," which is when a man explains a topic to a woman in a condescending, overconfident, and over-simplified manner as if she has no knowledge about the topic at hand

- Gender-specific roles in the home, such as men taking out the trash or mowing the lawn weekly while women take on daily tasks such as dishes and laundry

- Belittling or dismissing other people as insignificant, especially when expressing a sense of superiority

- Expectations of men being breadwinners, and when women are paid comparatively less for equivalent job responsibilities

- Treating sex as a competition, rather than an emotional connection with a partner

- Acting physically or verbally aggressive

- Not showing emotions or vulnerability and instead putting on a tough-guy exterior

- A sense of entitlement for being male

- Trying to control others through manipulation or bullying

Toxic masculinity has been noted to embody three core components: toughness, anti-femininity, and power. Toughness refers to the notion that men are strong, not weak, and will not back down. Aggression is part of toughness and is often encouraged as a sign of masculinity. Anti-femininity is the belief system that anything considered to be weak or emotional is a characteristic of a woman and therefore not acceptable for a "real man." Finally, power is the belief that a man is worthy of others' respect based solely on socioeconomic status.

Before discussing toxic masculinity with your child, I encourage you to explore at length some of your views and ideologies. Reflect on the roles they play in your life. Additionally, take note of how cultural dynamics, spiritual beliefs, family composition, financial status, and geographical location impact your view on masculinity. For example, perhaps you were raised in a household that remained steadfast to traditional gender norms. Although this might be a difficult task to engage in at first, it is vital for the conversation you will have with your child. If as a parent you are unaware of your own views, feelings, and emotions related to toxic masculinity, it will be difficult to be open and honest with your child.

When discussing toxic masculinity with your son, be vulnerable by sharing with him your feelings and emotions on this topic. Engage in conversation as to how toxic masculinity might play into his life. Lead a conversation about the expectations set forth in your home and the choices you are making as a family to break away from unhealthy cycles of toxic masculinity.

DEBUNKING THE RUMOR MILL:
DOESN'T TOXIC MASCULINITY ONLY HAVE A NEGATIVE IMPACT ON WOMEN?

Toxic masculinity negatively impacts women worldwide, but let's explore the many ways it also has a negative and damaging effect on your teen boy. Cultural, generational, and societal expectations are placed on your teen and the role he's supposed to fulfill in home, school, and social settings. Society sets certain expectations for teen boys, and when they don't fall into these stereotypical roles, they are sometimes bullied, ostracized, and made to feel inferior. As a parent to a teen boy, you have the power to influence your son to be sensitive to unhealthy attitudes about gender roles.

Toxic masculinity has a substantial negative effect on society, even financial deficits. A report from Promundo, a social services organization that promotes gender equality, finds that the steep cost of such toxic behaviors is upward of $15 billion in the United States each year and includes traffic accidents, suicide, depression, sexual assault, violence, and binge drinking. The financial impact is detrimental to us as a society. What would it look like to put a number on the emotional effects this could have on your male-identifying teen? The effects of toxic masculinity on teen boys are connected to depression, anxiety, sexual assault, and self-harming behaviors that include the use and abuse of drugs and alcohol.

What would you like your teen boy to learn about toxic masculinity and what it means to "be a man"? Take a moment to write down what you expect of your son at home: Is he supposed to be emotionally "strong" and suck it up, or is your son allowed to cry? Do you expect him to play sports, or is he encouraged to pursue any activities that interest him? Is he assigned the role of "man of the house," or is he given the green light to just be a kid? Is wearing makeup and/or nail polish frowned upon, or is he free to authentically express himself? Does your son have a skewed view of sex and physicality, or does he prioritize respect for other people's intellect and emotions?

In what ways do you want to debunk and break away from cycles that potentially lead to toxic masculinity with your son? Revisit your list, and ask yourself which characteristics your son displays are difficult for you to accept, even subconsciously as an emotional reaction. How do gender roles play into the upbringing of your child? Make it a family goal to break away from old patterns and create new and healthy ones. Have fun with it!

STUDY PREP: YOUR POSITIVE PARENTING NOTES

These are five easy ways to incorporate positive parenting in your household when it comes to common issues related to teen boys:

1. Set clear limits, rules, and expectations with your teenager. Hold firm on consequences, and concisely explain this to your son in age-appropriate words. Make sure he clearly understands the expectations you set for him and that you are both on the same page. If he does not follow your household rules, follow through with the consequences so they do not come off as empty threats. This teaches your son accountability for his behaviors and demonstrates that you consistently and reliably hold true to your word.

2. Identify the root of the problem. Why is your son acting out or being defiant? If you address the behavior but not the root causes, these situations will likely continue to occur repeatedly. Explore possible reasons, but not excuses, for his actions. This provides teachable moments in regard to emotional expression that is not overtly angry or inappropriate.

3. Allow for problem-solving. Engage your son in conversation as to his behaviors and actions versus telling him why he did it. Allow him to have a voice and ask him what is happening and what led to this reaction or action. Make sure your son is open to having a conversation and is not feeling forced or coerced into talking if he is not yet ready. It is okay to take some breathing room so that he can regulate himself before having a conversation.

4. Establish regular routines and sleep schedules. Yes, your teenager needs a bedtime! Invite him to be part of the conversation in establishing the routines that work best for him and fit your family. Schedules will shift as he gets older, but teens need an appropriate amount of sleep in order to perform well in school and other activities. Sit down and discuss the importance of sleep with him as well as what healthy sleep hygiene looks like. This can include limited screen time and a routine before bed, such as meditation or a warm bath to help him wind down.

5. Schedule intentional one-on-one time with your son. It can be as short as a ten-minute conversation or a full-on parent-son outing. Carve out a few minutes every day to let your son know he matters, is noticed, and is worthy of your time. Ask him how he wants to spend time together, and change it up occasionally. Regularly remind him of how important he is to your family and how much you enjoy spending time with him.

KEY TAKEAWAYS

After navigating the history of teenage boys, we now recognize the effects of positive parenting, breaking free from gender roles, and effective communication. Make note of the attitudes in your family based on toxic masculinity and cultural belief systems, and explore areas where your family would benefit from healthier viewpoints.

1. Implement positive parenting in everyday life by including the following elements:

   - Using open-ended questions. Implement intent when speaking with your child. Remember the effectiveness of speaking to him versus at him. Engage in back-and-forth conversation, avoiding punitive statements that might lead him to shut down.

   - Establishing firm rules. Set clear boundaries and expectations that are to be met in the home. Do what you say and say what you mean. Let your son know your expectations and the consequences for not following through.

   - Listening. When your child has a different view, perspective, or ideology than yours, create a space where he feels seen and heard. Validate his feelings and emotions. You can still set boundaries based on your expectations while allowing him to have his own point of view.

   - Problem-solving. Encourage your child to participate in the development of problem-solving skills. Talk a problem and solution through with him instead of giving him the answer.

   - Inquiring and exploring. Rather than assume, lead your teen son in a conversation about his feelings and reactions. Explore the possible root causes with him.

2. Break away from toxic masculinity. Leave behind the justi-
   fications and excuses for boys' behaviors and actions and
   hold them and yourself accountable.

3. Identify and set expectations on choices you make on
   gender roles within your family dynamic. Put into practice
   the choice of allowing your child to be who he feels comfortable being versus who he is "supposed to be" as a man.

4. Engage in conversation *with* your son rather than talking
   at him. Make sure listening and speaking are happening on
   both sides.

CHAPTER 2

THE DEVELOPMENT OF TEENAGE BOYS

This chapter addresses the biological changes that occur as a boy transitions into manhood. Hormones, especially testosterone, play key roles in puberty as boys develop into men, and it's true that there are differences in the biological timelines between male teens and female teens. In this chapter, we will also look at if and how testosterone plays a role in anger or aggression in teen boys. We will also explore the teenage brain and how its various stages of development can lead to risky behaviors. Mental health issues and their impact on teens will also be reviewed.

This all might sound heavy and overwhelming, but don't worry—we will navigate it together in a way that makes room for understanding and support. Positive parenting tips at the end of this chapter will help you continue to integrate changes in the interactions you have with your son.

The intention of this chapter is to provide you with a deeper understanding of your child and maybe even yourself. While reading this chapter you will learn a few key terms that play a role in your son's reactions, actions, and behaviors, including the following: frontal lobe, amygdala, the four F's, and window of tolerance.

Now let's dive in and take a journey through your teenager's development and the impact it has on his responses to you and others. Remember that this is a learning experience for you, so offer yourself kindness and grace.

HOW BOYS BECOME MEN

Teenage boys are typically seen as "moody, stinky, horny, lazy, irritable, and gross." What leads to these stereotypes? Let's look at the physiology and science behind how boys become men and the *why* behind some of these stereotypes and misconceptions. Testosterone and brain development in boys impact pubescent boys' actions and reactions during adolescence. During this time, teens are developing physical and social maturation while trying to figure out life along with daily pressures. Some of those pressures are placed on them by outside sources, whereas other pressures they put on themselves.

This is a difficult and risky time for your teen. He is walking through these changes while exploring sexual and physical maturity, learning the skills to become an adult, identifying and fine-tuning new developmental skills, determining autonomy from parents, and calibrating social ties with peers. This is not an easy feat!

Your son may be "stinky, gross, and lazy," which can be attributed to the physical and hormonal changes he is experiencing. His body is experiencing myriad changes, including hair growth, ejaculation, height and body shifts, and a deepening voice. He is trying to adapt to the physical changes. He may not completely understand them but likely feels uncomfortable reaching out to you to discuss this for fear of shame or embarrassment. He might be "moody and irritable" because he is attempting to process his feelings and emotions and what they mean. He is learning about and possibly questioning his identity and place in society, including who he is attracted to and possible implications based on cultural, societal, and familial expectations.

It is important to note that puberty timelines are different for teens assigned male at birth as opposed to their female counterparts. On average, teens assigned female at birth enter into the onset of puberty about two years before their male counterparts.

This plays a role in how men are treated by their counterparts and can also affect parenting, particularly if you are raising a teen son after having a teen daughter, who probably experienced puberty in a very different manner and age. "Boys are so immature," is commonly heard in middle school and high school hallways. Biologically, this is true! Boys mature at a slower rate than girls, and this impacts how they interact with parents and in social situations.

Despite all the stereotypes, boys typically have many positive qualities, such as intelligence, insightfulness, tenacity, humor, helpfulness, and kindness. It is important to remember your son's strengths while watching him walk through the difficulties and mood fluctuations of adolescence. You are in for quite the ride, so hold on tight!

WHAT HAPPENS WHEN YOU ADD $C_{19}H_{28}O_2$ (TESTOSTERONE) TO THE EQUATION

According to scientific studies, the average age for teen boys to go through puberty is between the ages of 10 and 14. However, this can occur as young as 9 and as old as 16. The release of the luteinizing hormone and the follicle-stimulating hormone into the bloodstream triggers the development of testosterone, which comes into play sometimes before a teen boy's physical changes are even recognizable. Although both boys and girls carry testosterone, it is the primary hormone in boys and the main hormone for the male reproductive system. Testosterone impacts puberty, bone mass, growth, metabolism, psychosocial status, and secondary sexual characteristics. Psychosocial status (social, cultural, and environmental factors that impact one's mind and behaviors) can impact your son, for example, if his puberty is delayed as compared to his peers or if he is developing ahead of his peers. Secondary sexual characteristics include increased body hair, such as facial and chest hair, and muscle mass generation.

As your teen son is going through these many physical, developmental, and emotional changes, this is also a very crucial time in your teen's development of self-esteem, self-worth, and identity formation. It's an exciting but scary time for teens and parents alike. Hormonal changes are difficult, and can leave your child feeling unsure of his decision-making process and confused about his own mood fluctuations. He is probably baffled by the bodily changes but is trying to maintain his cool, all while dealing with life's pressures. A strong support system with firm boundaries, compassion, and encouragement is vital.

Although your teen will likely come off as if he wants little to do with you—cue the mood swings!—this is an important time for you to provide a safe space to equip him with educational content in a way he prefers to absorb it, as well as offer ongoing support when he has questions. Your child will potentially present himself as annoyed with just about any substantive conversation, and that is absolutely okay and normal. Make conversations as pleasurable and light as you can while letting your son know you want to be supportive of him as he navigates his autonomy.

Set down your ground rules and expectations while also making room for feedback. Inquire about his needs and be prepared for "I don't know" answers from him. The importance of this conversation is to leave your son with accurate information about his puberty changes and an understanding that you are on his team and have his back.

DEBUNKING THE RUMOR MILL:
DOES TESTOSTERONE MAKE BOYS ANGRY OR MORE AGGRESSIVE?

Aggression can include verbal, emotional, or physical force with the intent to dominate or control another person. Testosterone has historically been made the excuse or application of causation for aggression in boys. Social media and movies perpetuate this belief by pointing to testosterone as the reason behind aggressive behaviors and mood. It fuels common misconceptions and misnomers as addressed in the first chapter, such as the misleading "boys will be boys" ideology (page 6).

When delving into the science behind hormones, and particularly testosterone, we find it is connected to competition, fear, and honor. It turns out testosterone is better connected to sex than aggression. Does this mean aggression is a biological response outside of a teen boy's capacity or control? One study notes that although there is a link between anger and testosterone, it is situationally induced, meaning it is a reaction to the anger rather than the cause of it. Ultimately, although testosterone and aggression are loosely linked, studies confirm it is a minimal connection.

So, how does testosterone affect your teenager and his perceived aggressive moods or reactions? Although aggression is not completely correlated to testosterone, there is a connection to primal survival. Testosterone is one component in the role hormones play in your teen's actions. Although much research has been conducted on this topic, it is crucial to note the inconsistencies in results.

Although many studies continue to show a low correlation between testosterone and aggression, typical puberty involves average or normal values of testosterone that exclude high-dose testosterone's connection to aggression. High doses of testosterone outside of a normal range can come from the use of anabolic steroids or medical issues that impact a child's hormone levels. If this is the case for your child, please seek medical attention and professional support for him.

A LOOK INSIDE THE TEENAGE BRAIN

The teen brain is a complex one. Not only is it going through the social and emotional evolution of becoming an adult, but also the brain is still developing, which adds to the complications of adolescence. This process is spread throughout childhood, youth, and young adulthood, ranging from ages 9 to 25. This is not only a time for brain development but also self-exploration, new insights, and awareness.

Neuroscientists have determined that the teen brain does not function at the same capacity of a fully developed adult. Evidence shows a teen brain's processes, perceptions, and responses are unique and unlike an adult's brain. Teens process information through a different part of the brain than adults do. Adults have full use of their frontal lobes compared to adolescents, and we will address this further in the next section. Teens, alternatively, utilize the amygdala to process information and emotions.

The amygdala is the part of the brain that is responsible for several key functions for humans. Its main job is to regulate emotions, primarily fear and aggression. It is also the reward center and includes pleasure seeking. Additionally, it is responsible for "flight, fight, freeze, or fawn." This is also known as the four F's, which are common responses to trauma. Trauma is defined as "the response to a deeply distressing or disturbing event that overwhelms an individual's ability to cope, causes feelings of helplessness, diminishes their sense of self and their ability to feel a full range of emotions and experiences." Any event that creates a disruption in a person's life and causes dysregulation can be considered traumatic.

Our "window of tolerance," originally developed at UCLA by Dr. Dan Siegel, plays a huge role in the way the four F's appear as reactions to trauma. The window of tolerance is best described as a safety zone where a person has the most capacity to process emotions and function in daily life. This zone can decrease in the event of a traumatic experience, leading to a higher likelihood of the four F's coming into play. When our safety zone is decreased, our body and brain go into dysregulation, which leads to hypo- or hyperarousal . . . and the four F's.

These are some examples of how the four F's are broken down in terms of actions, feelings, reactions, and behaviors:

- FIGHT: angry outburst, aggression, grumpiness, irritability, need to control, explosive behaviors, poor impulse control, bullying

- FLIGHT: overthinking, anxiety, panic, avoidance, worry, difficulty sitting still, perfectionism

- FREEZE: difficulty making decisions, shutting down, numbness, depression, disassociation, isolating behaviors

- FAWN: people pleasing, poor boundaries, codependency, difficulty saying no, feeling overwhelmed, avoiding conflict

RULE OF THUMB: THEIR FRONTAL LOBE IS (ALMOST) ALWAYS THE CULPRIT

Although your teenager has capacity and use of his frontal lobe, the frontal lobe does not fully develop until about 25 years of age. Because the frontal lobe oversees rationality and executive functioning, this explains a lot of teenage behaviors. As noted earlier in this chapter, teens are utilizing more of the amygdala portion of the brain, which can lead to risky and sometimes impulsive behaviors.

This is a crucial time for a teen to learn to control his emotions, balance the differences between right and wrong, work on decision-making skills, and process cause-and-effect relationships. Because your son's frontal lobe is still developing to full capacity, he is more likely to make decisions based on impulse or emotion rather than rational thought. Studies find that frontal lobe growth does not refer to size but rather increased connectivity between brain regions.

Peer pressure plays a huge role in a teenager's life, and frontal lobe capacity is a big reason for this! Although this is a scary thought, you also get to witness and guide your child into healthy decision-making skills that will lead him to successfully transition into adulthood. It might be difficult for your teen to understand or hear about brain development, but it is fundamental in creating a plan to aid your child in building the cognitive skills needed as he evolves into adulthood.

Suggestions for you to create this plan include continued expectations, boundaries, and rules set forth in the home setting. Have open conversations about peer pressure, underage drinking, what constitutes risky behaviors, and the consequences of engaging in such behavior. If your child engages in behavior that's deemed exceptionally risky, help him problem solve and allow this to become a corrective experience rather than a punitive one. This way he's more likely to reach out to you when he finds himself in a jam. That being said, you should still show him the consequences of his actions. Praise him and thank him when he shows enough trust in you to contact you when facing a scary or dangerous situation.

DEBUNKING THE RUMOR MILL:
ARE TEENS MORE AT RISK FOR MENTAL HEALTH STRUGGLES THAN ADULTS?

This can be a loaded question, as mental health impacts us all regardless of age. However, several factors place your teen at risk for mental health struggles more so than adults. As discussed earlier in this chapter, your child's frontal lobe is still under construction. Also noted in the previous chapter is that social media and social status comes with added pressures that can lead to issues that affect your child's self-esteem, sense of worth, and emotional state. Studies conclude that older adolescents ranging from ages 17 to 18 are twice as likely to develop a mood disorder than are teens at 13 or 14 years of age.

When observing adolescence as a whole, we can divide it into four subcategories and each includes unique characteristics and life events that can contribute to mental health struggles. The pressure your son might feel to perform or keep up to par with societal demands can impact his feelings of self-worth, self-esteem, and identity. This in turn can lead to depression, anxiety, substance use, or other mental health struggles.

→ Ages 9 to 12 (Preteen/Tween): During this period of time, your son starts to develop into puberty. He is learning to navigate from being seen as a child and looking toward being a teenager. Some physical and hormonal changes might occur, and he is dealing with the confusion of how to manage the weird emotions and sensations he's feeling due to his increases in testosterone.

→ Ages 13 to 16 (Young Adolescence): During this stage, your child is in the full swing of puberty and has experienced many physical changes, including changes in his voice, weight, height, and body hair.

→ Ages 17 to 18 (Older Adolescence): This is both an exciting and scary time of maturity for an older adolescent, although he is not expected to perform and react as a full-on legal adult. Although he has not yet formed the necessary skills through his brain development, societal expectations and demands continue.

continued >>

> Ages 19 to 25 (Young Adults): At this point in a young man's life, he has the societal expectations of having finished high school and is likely entering the workforce or military or is continuing his educational journey at the university, trade, or community college level.

STUDY PREP: YOUR POSITIVE PARENTING NOTES

Implementing positive parenting may seem like a daunting task after reading through all of the information provided, but remember all the skills you have already acquired since chapter 1. Practice and consistency are key when incorporating positive parenting. Positive parenting has also been linked to promoting healthy development of the adolescent brain.

Five easy ways to incorporate positive parenting in your household during your teen son's development include the following:

1. Have realistic expectations. Recognize your child's developmental, emotional, and physical capacity, taking a strength-based approach to setting realistic expectations for him, playing up and connecting him to his natural strengths and talents. Set him up for success over failure by setting concise and specific expectations. Categorize his capacity based on his age and developmental stage, determining how you want to provide your son with autonomous decision-making within the expectations set forth in your home. For context, remember the development of his frontal lobe is not fully formed until age 25. This does not mean you coddle him, but instead guide him into consistent and responsible choices while challenging

his thought process. Set attainable goals and chores—a 13-year-old does not have the same capacity and ability as a 17-year-old.

2. Create a positive learning environment. You are the guide as your child continues to develop his problem-solving skills. Implement an environment that allows for him to feel your warmth, kindness, and love. Guide, encourage, and teach him in ways that feel supportive and uplifting. Praise your son for allowing himself to engage in conversations with you about topics that are probably uncomfortable for him. Make it clear to him that he can come to you with anything—no question is considered dumb or silly.

3. Build self-confidence. Positive affirmations and praise are key components to positive parenting. Whether your son is 9 or 19, he will continue to benefit and grow from the use of these strategies. Positive affirmations aid in the development of self-confidence, therefore allowing his inner voice to become strong. Praise serves up a standard of validating and reinforcing expectations in the home. Remember that your child is still primarily utilizing the amygdala—his brain's reward center—for problem-solving and processing information. Therefore, praise is stored, and positive behavior patterns are more likely to continue.

HERE ARE FOUR TIPS TO IMPLEMENT PRAISE:

a. Label your praise by being specific about what you appreciate.

b. Praise even the baby steps and minor achievements.

c. Praise the actions you want to see continue.

d. Praise verbally and also physically with hugs and high-fives.

4. Take time apart. There is no doubt that parenting is not always easy! In some instances, time apart is best for both you and your son. This teaches your child that it's okay to take a break when things feel overwhelming. It creates space between you and your child when his actions, reactions, behaviors, and possible defiance become too much to bear. Identify the need for a break, set a timeline, and come back to the topic at hand when you both have had the space to collect yourselves after a difficult interaction.

5. Establish positive reinforcements. Positive reinforcement is a form of discipline that allows open and effective communication to ensue between you and your son. It encourages you to take an approach that highlights your son's individual strengths and qualities and builds on them. Rather than harping on what he's done wrong, show great appreciation for all the things that he does well. This will boost his self-esteem and empower him.

KEY TAKEAWAYS

In this chapter, you gained the knowledge of testosterone's impact on your child's actions and reactions. Determine how to implement this information into the dynamic of your parent-son relationship as he develops problem-solving skills and full use of his frontal lobe. You have also acquired knowledge on the development of the teen brain, and the importance of your guidance and support during his adolescence and into adulthood.

1. Testosterone is not the sole hormone responsible for your son's mood. Although it does play a role in his mood and behaviors it is important to note that it is only one of the many hormones that are affecting the changes that are happening in him during puberty.

2. Teach your child about his window of tolerance and the four F's (flight, fight, freeze, and fawn) in an age-appropriate manner. Support him in identifying how and when he engages in these trauma responses. Support him in creating an awareness of what increases his window of tolerance, also known as his safety zone. This will empower him and also teach him how and why he reacts the way he does to certain triggers.

3. Your son is still developing full use of his frontal lobe. This is a crucial time for you to be a source of guidance and support. This is a great teaching opportunity for implementing healthy coping and problem-solving skills. Remember, your child is learning from you—your actions, choices, and behaviors will play key roles in his development.

4. Normalize mental health and the need for external support. Create a safe space in your home that invites your child to verbalize his need or desire for mental health services without feeling that there is something "wrong" with him.

CHAPTER 3

BECOMING FLUENT IN TEENAGE BOY

In this chapter, we will discuss how teens communicate. Teens have their own language riddled with slang, memes, and complexities that make it unique. Here we will punctuate the importance of communication and implementation of skills that allow your child to engage in effective conversation with you. The process of adolescence and puberty impact your child's communication skills and style. Exercising patience during this time will be pivotal in continuing to foster a healthy relationship with your teen son.

Throughout this chapter, we will also address why teens communicate in the way they do and how it is a normal part of their adolescence. We will discuss social media—both its positives and negatives—utilizing research to address the impact it has on your adolescent's behavior, moods, and risk-taking behaviors. Social media apps and dialect will be dissected in order to provide you with a deeper understanding of how your child communicates with peers and others in the cyber world.

We will discuss the implementation of open-ended questions and classify the differences between them and closed-ended questions. We will also delve into Erikson's stages of development and the role they play in your son's communication. Throughout this chapter, we will apply research evidence on how to become fluent in teenage boy. Although each teen boy has his own uniqueness, a general guideline can be used to aid communication with teenage boys.

HOW TEENAGE BOYS COMMUNICATE

Communication with teenagers can be difficult. They have their own unique language full of slang and individualities that are not relevant to adults. At times, it might even feel like your son is speaking a foreign language—and in some ways he is. Historically, teens have devised unique words to express themselves within groups. For example, the 1960s were "groovy" and "far-out, man," and you can probably think of several slang terms that bring you back to your own formative years. Today's teen slang is even further complicated by acronyms that are used while texting.

These are some common terms currently being used by today's teens: "snatched," "extra," "big yikes," "flex," "no cap," "low key," "high key," "I'm dead," "slay," "straight fire," "spill the tea," "CD9," "shook," "Netflix and chill," "curve," "LMIRL," "POS," "sus," "lit," "GOAT," "Karen," "bae," "fleek," "FOMO," "bye Felicia," "big mad," "diamond hands," and "mittens." Now although you are probably left scratching your head, it is important to recognize the verbiage your teen is using, particularly around his peers. Educate yourself by researching the meanings of these and other slang terms.

In addition to the slang integrated into teen communication, there are also key differences in the ways male teens communicate as opposed to female teens. A study conducted in 2011 notes that boys were more likely than girls to take a self-taught approach to picking up communication skills, learning them by experience rather than being taught by someone else. In this same study, it was found that the male teens surveyed displayed more confidence than female teens when communicating with authority figures. Those male teens also displayed more concern about the social implications of communication. Still, communication between teen boys varies depending on who's on the other side of the conversation. Conversation is vastly different with male peers, female peers, adults, and other authority figures.

Allow your child the freedom to express his beliefs and thoughts in a welcoming setting. Approach conversations from a curious and nonjudgmental standpoint. Validating and respecting his views and thoughts increases communication and fosters a more positive interaction. It lets your child recognize his right to his views, opinions, and beliefs. Additionally, it helps shape his communication skills so he becomes an effective and mature adult who is able to engage in active listening and speaking.

Engaging in physical activities, such as walking or playing basketball, is beneficial when engaging in conversation with your son. Boys are generally spatial thinkers, which means they think best when engaged in an activity or movement. When engaging with peers, it is important for them to be accepted. Teens adjust their tone, style, and interests based on those around them. Peer pressure and acceptance are highly important during adolescence. Teen boys begin to identify ways to develop self-identity autonomous from the parental unit. This is a time when your son is exploring his likes and dislikes and forming opinions independently.

THE IMPORTANCE OF COMMUNICATING ABOUT FEELINGS

As we continue to shift away from toxic masculinity, we want to encourage teen boys to engage in open, healthy, and effective communication. This is not an easy accomplishment as teens are, many times, wrapped up in their own worlds. Pressures they face include school, social media status, connections with friends and romantic partners, bodily changes, and the pressures to perform in activities such as sports or debate club.

It is important to note that as they grow through adolescence, some teens will become broody, quiet, and reserved. This is a normal part of the adolescent process, and it is addressed further in the next section. During this time, your role as a parent is key in creating a safe space for communication to flow freely. Your boy is learning how to effectively communicate his feelings, thoughts, and emotions, so determine what you want that to look like for your son. Make him part of the conversation and build an open-communication plan together. Discuss rules, guidelines, and expectations at home, but remind him that his voice matters and that you want to be a support system for him. Be someone he can come to for advice or a venting session.

According to Erikson's stages of psychosocial development, a theory introduced in the 1950s, adolescence is when your child is experiencing Stage 5: Identity vs. Role Confusion, which occurs during ages 12 through 18. It's theorized that during this stage, your child is learning to develop and identify his sense of self. This is the stage in which he forms his unique identity based on his life priorities—family, friends, romantic relationships, school, career.

This is also a time of confusion as he moves toward self-actualization and identity formation, so it is important to provide him with space to explore his sense of self and how he fits into society. To support your child is to provide him with a space to express himself, validate his feelings, give him trust and praise, and be observant of any changes in his mood or behaviors. In addition, make sure you are giving him privacy but balance that with engaging in and keeping up with his interests. Let him know you respect his private space—please, knock on the door before entering his room—while engaging in curious conversation about his interests in music, TV shows, games, sports, and so on.

DEBUNKING THE RUMOR MILL:
MY SON ONLY RESPONDS WITH ONE-WORD ANSWERS, DOES THIS MEAN HE'S UPSET WITH ME?

Your son responding with one-word answers is completely normal. He is a typical moody, brooding teenager. He is experiencing a plethora of physical, emotional, and societal changes—not to mention the continued development of his frontal lobe. During this period of transition, boys often become more reclusive and silent. That means getting one-word answers. Also be aware of body language. Identify what his body language looks like and the means to determine when and how to best approach him.

The utilization of open-ended questions is very important when communicating with anyone, but particularly with tweens and teens. A frequent response to common questions is, "I dunno," which can feel rude, dismissive, or downright infuriating. Stay away from questions that are considered close-ended and instead opt for open-ended questions that demand a more thoughtful response. Here are some samples of close-ended and open-ended questions:

CLOSE-ENDED: These types of questions don't require much thought and can be answered with one word.

1. "How was your day?"

2. "Did you have a good day?"

3. "Are you doing okay today?"

4. "What's wrong?"

5. "Is your homework done?"

6. "Are you hungry?"

OPEN-ENDED: The following questions are thought-provoking and offer room for a teen to elaborate on the topic.

1. "What was your favorite part of your day today?"

2. "What are the things that make you most happy?"

3. "What do you like most about your friends?"

4. "What is your favorite family tradition and why?"

continued >>

5. "Who are your favorite teachers, and what do you like most about them?"

6. "What are some things you would like to see change in our home?"

Although some of these open-ended questions could still elicit the infamous "I dunno," be patient with your child as you venture into new forms of communication. His response could genuinely mean he doesn't know or is undecided. It could also mean he has never been asked this type of question before, he is trying to push you away, or he feels like he is on the spot or that it's none of your business.

Don't push or pry. Exert patience and kindness when engaging in open-ended conversation. These questions are not meant to feel like an interrogation but rather a flow of conversation between two people. Create an environment in which your child does not feel ambushed or pressured. If he is slow to open up to you, encourage him by letting him know you are excited to chat more about his life when he is ready.

UNDERSTANDING THE DIFFERENT SOCIAL MEDIA DIALECTS

The many options on the internet and social media apps open up many new avenues of communication among teens. Gone are the days of Facebook, which teens view as social media for "old people." The new wave has come in hard with Instagram, Snapchat, Twitter, and TikTok. In a sea of social media apps, teens are now able to communicate with more than just simple texts.

"Finsta" is slang for a fake Instagram account that is used to communicate and post on their "real life," which they want to hide from parents and family members.

Teens can utilize apps such as Discord and WhatsApp for memes, videos, emojis, picture sharing, and group chats. Members can create public and private groups and chat with any member they choose to connect with. It is important to discuss rules and regulations of use of the above-mentioned apps with your child as well as the appropriateness of content that is placed on the internet. Many times, this is a way teens choose to communicate with their peers and others on social media as a way of protecting their privacy from parents. Although you want to encourage individuality and decision-making skills, it is also important to discuss the repercussions and dangers lurking online through some of these apps. Cyberbullying, data breaches, exposure to inappropriate content, and potential for human trafficking are risks that come with social media apps.

With the help of social media, teens can connect with real-life and virtual friends. Some of the benefits of social media include an increased connection with peers as well as exploring creativity and varied interests. Many educational institutions now utilize the internet as a way to provide support, connect with students, and encourage learning though the virtual world. Social media also allows your child to connect with local and global news and information, so he can gain further understanding of issues and history that is occurring around him—but does he know how to ascertain which sources are reliable and those that are not?

It is imperative to discuss the benefits and risks with your child as well as limits and regulations that they are agreeing to abide by. Some topics of conversation might include your expectations of his social media use, staying safe, privacy settings, not connecting with people he does not know in real life, coming to you for any concerns or questions, and avoiding clicking on pop-up ads that can lead to spyware or take him to unsafe sites.

THE PRESSURES TO PERFORM ON SOCIAL MEDIA

Social media has become the most acceptable form of communication among teens. We live in a world of *likes* and followers, and that enhances a teenager's social status. Social media is now the easiest and fastest way to relay information to multiple people at once. Information and photos of a friend, enemy, or romantic interest are now accessible at the click of a button. Social media is the easiest way for teens to connect with friends and receive validation.

The number of views and *likes* on a story, post, or video often determines their feelings of worth and status among peers. This creates obsessive-like behaviors. Teens engage in daily life events and moments to capture the "perfect post" rather than enjoying in-the-moment interactions with friends and family. Even a teen's alone time might be overshadowed with taking selfie photos or posting videos. The need for *likes* and online validation can negatively impact self-esteem and self-worth. Teens develop dependency on the comments received. This can be a double-edged sword as comments can quickly facilitate between praise and negative criticism. The effect of negativity and cyberbullying on your child can be devastating and even severely impact his mental health.

Take note of your teen's utilization of social media and the impact it has. Although there are studies that indicate an increase in high-risk behaviors for teens on social media, it is important to point out that not all social media activity is bad. For some teens, it is an expressive outlet where they feel seen, heard, and understood. For some teens, social media is a way to connect with others, especially when dealing with an illness, exploring their sexual identity, or handling isolation such as that during the recent pandemic.

Some of the potential negative impacts on your child might be associated with depression, anxiety, low self-esteem, and loneliness. Unrealistic expectations of status, physical attributes, and friend count can adversely influence your child's psyche. Peer pressure can also lead your son to engage in cyberbullying as a way to fit in with others. For your son's well-being, consider setting limits on and monitoring social media usage, and have an open dialogue about social media use, acceptable content, and appropriate interactions online. Listen to your child when he tells you about his social media needs and desires. Engage in a collaborative effort to set forth a healthy and balanced plan for him.

DEBUNKING THE RUMOR MILL:
ARE TEENS USING CERTAIN SOCIAL MEDIA APPS TO SEND INAPPROPRIATE CONTENT?

Snapchat, Instagram, WhatsApp, and Discord are some of the apps teens use to exchange inappropriate content among themselves. One of the biggest concerns with social media apps is teens engaging in "sexting." Sexting, also known as "sex texting," is sending a message or image that is sexually explicit or suggestive in nature. It can include words, pictures, and videos that portray partial or full nudity as well as sexual acts. One of the fears parents have is that once these images are in cyberspace they will live there for eternity.

Past studies have concluded that there is a higher prevalence of inappropriate content being shared through the use of social media apps. A 2020 study reports that teens who engage in the use of social media are more likely to partake in sexting and other high-risk behaviors. Both sexting and self-harm (non-suicidal self-injury) were found to be connected to social media use. It is important to note that there is also an increased risk of these behaviors when

continued >>

teens regularly use four or more social media apps. On average kids and teens ages 8 to 19 spend an average of seven hours a day on screen time, including use of the computer, phone, and television.

Additional behaviors associated with use of social media apps include higher risk of alcohol consumption. It is also notable that there is a correlation to obesity, cardiovascular risk, decreased sleep, quality of sleep, depression, and anxiety. Keep in mind that risky behavior is already a part of adolescence, and teens are going to take unnecessary risks because they are utilizing the amygdala, which is associated with impulse and instinctive behavior. Research further indicates that male teens have a higher likelihood of engaging in cyberbullying.

However, it is also important to note that studies indicate that the use of prosocial media can benefit your teen. Prosocial media is any form of media that promotes generous behaviors, including helping others, generosity, and friendly demeanors. Some studies report that prosocial media can create a positive impact in teens. However, teens will require more than just prosocial media to create altruistic behaviors. This is a great area where you can foster your child's maturity and enhance positive experiences through social media and real-life situations by modeling positive behaviors in the home setting.

STUDY PREP: YOUR POSITIVE PARENTING NOTES

Five easy ways to incorporate positive parenting in your household when it comes to communicating with your teenager include the following:

1. Establish consequences. Set specific rules and regulations as well as consequences for not complying with the established rules. Allow your child to be part of the conversation of what the rules and expectations are at home. Rules should be definable, understandable, reasonable, and enforceable. Reasonable rules should be put in place based on your child's capacity and developmental stage. Establish rules that are enforceable and that you are willing to commit to.

2. Use the if/then rule. Let your child know how privileges are earned and be clear and concise with your rules. Make sure you set achievable expectations for your child. For example, consider the following: "*If* you finish all of your homework, *then* you can play an hour of video games or go out with your friends." Determine the *then* portion based on your child's developmental stage, motivation, and interests. The if/then rule allows for a child to learn and earn privileges. It creates a healthy dynamic of expectations and positive reinforcement.

3. Avoid manipulation. When your child does not meet the rules that are set, chances are high that he will try to manipulate his way out of consequences. Your child will likely start the negotiations with you and present his case as to why he feels that he should not have to abide by the rules. Remember the rule of thumb we have established in previous chapters: Do what you say and say what you mean.

Nevertheless, allow him to express his reasoning, and validate him for it. But also remind him that the rules are put in place for a reason and that consequences are a natural part of his choices and actions taken. Note that there will be rare occasions where something might actually have been outside of your child's control. This is a rare exception and not typically the rule when it comes to manipulation. Ask yourself what standard you want to set with him.

4. Model appropriate behavior. This is a critical time in your son's life. He is learning how to make good choices and solve problems. You are the example he is following, whether or not he makes it overtly known. Recognize that your approach to proceeding with difficult decisions is being modeled for your child.

5. Do not be overly critical. Puberty is a fragile time for your child's self-esteem, so he will be more sensitive to criticism—even if you feel you are being constructive. Don't make fun of him, even if you are making light of a situation. Total acceptance is a dire need for your son. Sit with him and encourage him to freely and honestly process his feelings, thoughts, and emotions. Rather than using a critical statement such as, "It's about time that you got a B in Science! I was wondering if that would ever happen," instead be supportive with something along the lines of "Great job getting a B! I am so proud of you."

KEY TAKEAWAYS

We are now able to identify that adolescents have a unique way of communicating. One-word responses are perfectly normal for them during puberty. Social media plays an important role in your teen's life and has both positive and negative associations. It is a good idea to keep up with social media apps, particularly those your child prefers. Understanding their lingo and slang will also create awareness for you as to some of the behaviors and activities he is engaging in.

Keep in mind that slang and apps are consistently evolving; therefore, make sure you keep up. You can set rules and expectations on the use of these apps as well as consequences for not following the rules. Include your child in conversations on setting rules and expectations in your home. Discuss rules and be open to reevaluating them with your child as he continues to grow and gets older.

- Open-ended questions are a key factor in communication with your teen. Stay away from questions that only require a one-word response.

- Encourage emotional expression from your teen son. Consistently banish cycles of toxic masculinity from your home.

- Provide a safe and nurturing environment for your child to express himself and ensure you are providing a safe space. Do not make fun of him, even if you are attempting to make light of a difficult situation.

- Patience will be your greatest virtue during this bumpy ride of adolescence. There will be times when you will need a time out from your son—it is okay to take it.

CHAPTER 4

THE SOCIAL LIVES OF TEENAGE BOYS

In this chapter we will peel back the layers of the social life of a teenage boy, including the importance of strong male relationships on your son's development. Integrating diversity and inclusivity in the friendships he forms will have a meaningful impact on his growth, so addressing racial and cultural issues is also important as your child forms his understanding of integration versus exclusion. We will also touch on peer pressure and bullying in friendships, and this is also a time in your child's life when he is exploring his sexuality, including gender identity and orientation. Dating will come into his life, so discussing rules, expectations, and consent with your child is key as he starts developing romantic interests.

You can also begin having conversations about sexual activity and safe sex. You can have a conversation with him about your concerns about his engaging in sexual activity and also encourage him to come to you with any questions in regard to safe sex, STDs, mutual consent, or pressure to engage in sexual activity if he is not yet ready to do so. Although this might be an uncomfortable thought for you, it is necessary to recognize that sexuality is part of puberty and that ignoring the topic won't make it go away.

We will also delve into what it looks like if your son dates someone you don't like and how you can discuss this with him in a way that does not push him away but instead inspires him to make his own decisions while respecting the rules and expectations you've set forth as a parent.

THE IMPORTANCE OF STRONG MALE FRIENDSHIPS

Establishing strong meaningful relationships with male peers is especially important during your son's adolescence. During this time, his friendships provide a sense of belonging to and fitting in with groups of people other than family members. Slightly older peers can also be a resource for advice and support. As your child is navigating through adolescence, he will want a sense of independence and will create an emotional separation from you while also forging closer bonds with his friends. They are all navigating a similar journey and are a strong support system to one another.

He is exploring his identity through independence and building on his self-esteem. He spends more time with his friends because he feels seen, heard, and understood by others who are also facing the pressures of adolescence. In their younger years, teens will likely bond with friends based on similar interests. In older adolescence, teens will also find connections through commonalities in values, beliefs, educational interests, and social-ization similarities. Teens are looking for loyalty, commitment, genuineness, intimacy, and common values.

Formulating and strengthening these relationships create positive impacts on your child during his adolescence and into adulthood. During this period in your son's life, he is learning, growing, and evolving as he continues to gain knowledge and take on additional roles and responsibilities. He is learning to problem solve and is starting to date, transitioning from middle school to high school, learning to drive, and making decisions about life after graduation. His friendships during this time not only will provide support but often are also contributing factors to the decisions and choices he is making.

There are three main components that play a role in his friendships: the relationship dynamic with parents, the development of identity, and entering into romantic relationships. During middle adolescence, your teen will be more inclined to spend more of his time with same-sex peers. As he continues into older adolescence, this shifts to opposite-sex peers. Teens will also begin spending more time with peers in extracurricular and social situations as opposed to just school settings.

The time spent together with friends plays a significant role in teen development as they learn to be in relationships outside of family life and dynamics. They begin to explore and develop a sense of loyalty, intimacy, belonging, and understanding that they don't necessarily have with adults in their lives. Your teen's peers will create an impact on his choices, decisions, school accomplishments, and problem-solving. Due to the impact and significance of friendships during this time, it is important to be aware of your son's group of friends and what bonds them. His friends help shape and foster your son's self-worth and identity.

A DIVERSE FRIEND GROUP IS ALSO KEY

Strong friendships are important for your son and should be encouraged. It is of equal importance to foster the growth of his friendships across ethnicities, race, gender identities, and orientations. Although race and ethnicity are interrelated, they are not the same. Race is viewed as biological differences, including characteristics and skin color, which are typically divided into five groups: 1) American Indian or Alaska Native, 2) Asian, 3) Black or African American, 4) Native Hawaiian or other Pacific Islander, and 5) white. Ethnicity is defined as cultural expression and identity.

Gender identity and orientation can also be combined but have stark differences. Gender identity can include sex assigned at birth as well as the gender with which a person identifies. Gender orientation is viewed as a person's sexual preference, such as straight, gay, queer, or pansexual.

By supporting and encouraging diversity in friendships you break away from toxic masculinity belief systems and encourage inclusivity. The integrations of diversity and inclusion create a learning space for your child to build upon kindness, acceptance, empathy, and leadership. Research indicates that those in educational settings show better academic and social skills when engaging in cross-cultural and diverse friendships.

Opportunity for diverse friendships is largely influenced by accessibility to diverse peers. A teen's understanding and views on diversity in relationships play significant roles in the formations of these relationships. Views are formulated based on values and belief systems implemented in the home setting as well as social media influences. As with same-sex friendships, similarities in interests and values help define diversified friendships.

Toxic masculinity and belief systems impact your son's ability and willingness to develop and engage in friendships with other teens who have differing sexual orientations and gender identities. Recognize homophobia or other belief systems that might impair or blur your son's ability to engage with teens who are not of the same orientation or identity.

An example of this might be if your son were to say, "He's too much of a sissy for me to be friends with him. What would people think of me?" What you teach in your home is reflective of his choices. Willingness to integrate diversity in his life creates greater opportunity for growth, understanding, and awareness. This also helps your son as he transitions into adulthood and becomes acquainted with different personalities as he grows in his socialization skills.

DEBUNKING THE RUMOR MILL: I HEARD THAT ONE OF MY SON'S FRIENDS IS A BAD INFLUENCE. WHAT SHOULD I DO?

As your child begins to develop his personality and autonomy, he will probably be attracted to like-minded peers. Although this is not always the case, it is typically the norm. Therefore, it is important to maintain consistent boundaries, limits, and expectations with him. Have open dialogue about his friendships, asking about his friends and what bonds they share. Your son is surrounding himself with others that he accepts and feels comfortable with.

At some point, your son will likely have at least one friend you don't like. Criticizing or speaking ill of his friend will only further ostracize you and strengthen their bond, so approach this situation delicately. Inform your child occasionally and not repetitively of your disapproval and the reasons behind it with clear and concise "I" statements: "I am uncomfortable with your friendship with Jonathan, because I notice he doesn't value a good grade-point average as much as you do." Let that sink in and allow him to utilize his decision-making skills. The more you push against Jonathan, the more he will want to be around this person. Take note of the differences in your son's mood, attitude, behaviors, and reactivity when spending time with this peer. Set limits and boundaries when it comes to behaviors that are acceptable in your home.

When observing different groups of male adolescent friends, it is noted that the status of one member of the group can create a hierarchy where the other teens are more likely to fall in line with the perceived leader's actions,

continued >>

behaviors, and responses. Status is a key factor in patterns of teasing and mockery. Teens desire to be accepted and will fall in line with the perceived group leader in order to prevent being an outcast or bullied when they just want to belong.

Promoting positive behaviors is a great way to encourage your child to seek out peers who will have a more positive impact on him. Identify what your child's interests and commonalities are with the "bad influence." It will be important to note if your child is like-minded, has similar interests, is looking to belong, or feels the need to engage in poor choices to fit in.

DATING IS HEALTHY (AND NOT ALWAYS JUST ABOUT SEX)

As your teen begins to explore his sexuality, dating will be a topic of conversation in your home. Sit down with your son and discuss your rules, values, beliefs, and expectations that you have of and for him when it comes to dating. This might also be the time your son is identifying his sexual identity and orientation. Have a candid, open, and nonjudgmental conversation with him, acknowledging that this is an uncomfortable subject matter for all parties involved.

Prior to sitting down with your child, it is important for you to create an awareness of your biases, protective mechanisms, and ideas of sexuality and orientation. Be prepared to answer his questions with thoughtfulness and honesty. Recognize that this is a vulnerable time for you and him as you accept the idea of your son's maturing romantic interests. Dating and romance are integral parts of adolescence and important components to his overall development and growth.

It is important to note when to have this conversation with your son. Romantic interests or crushes can start developing from ages 10 to 14 when tweens and teens are considering intimate relationships with opposite- or same-sex partners. Crushes are more likely to occur in early adolescence, whereas full-on relationships will play a more pivotal role in middle and older adolescence, around 15 to 20 years of age. Crushes can also be one-sided, and mutual consent is a great topic to begin discussing with your teen during this time. Have a conversation about what consent means and how it applies to a potential crush or partner.

Dating has many different components. It is a time for your child to explore his romantic interests and develop patterns of communication and relationship dynamics. During this time, your teen will likely engage in some form of intimacy with his romantic partner. Although not all relationships will lead to a sexually intimate relationship, there is a possibility of it occurring. Sexuality develops over time, and this is a time of exploration for your teen in regard to their sexual identity and romantic interests.

As noted earlier, this is an important time to discuss mutual consent. It is also of equal importance to discuss safe sex, STDs, and birth control with your teen. You will also want to discuss healthy relationships and lead a conversation about what that means to him. Provide him with a relaxed environment while allowing him to express his views on intimate relationships. This is also a suitable time to provide him with examples of healthy versus toxic relationships.

With the fun of exploring new and exciting romantic relationships comes the risk of breakups. Relationships will end, and it will feel devastating for your child. Remember to provide a space that doesn't feel suffocating. Keep an eye on your child's mood, actions, and behavior. Breaking up is hard, so grant him kindness, grace, and patience.

BEING A GOOD FRIEND ISN'T UNLIKE BEING A GOOD BOYFRIEND

As your son continues to explore his friendships and romantic relationships, have a conversation with him about what constitutes a good friend and romantic partner. Remember that what he sees at home in regard to your friendships and romantic relationships will influence his take on his friendships and partnerships. Together you can create awareness for him of what his needs and desires are in friendships and other relationships. This can be an amazing learning experience for him where he is learning to recognize reciprocity in relationships.

Have a conversation with him about what you appreciate about your friendships, such as loyalty, trust, kindness, understanding, and common interests, and what you expect in a romantic partnership, which might have some overlapping qualities. This is also a great time to discuss the importance of a sense of friendship within a romantic relationship. Although physical and sexual attraction are big factors in romantic relationships, it is also important to identify commonalities such as trust and core values that deepen intimacy with a romantic partner.

Your child's friendships provide a healthy platform for him to learn how to communicate, compromise, and build trust and stability with peers. This will play a pivotal role in how your child continues to develop these skills in a romantic relationship. Identify what you want your child to learn about when it comes to expressing his needs in a relationship and also share what respect for others' boundaries and views looks like. This is important in both friendships and relationships as he is learning to explore views and beliefs that may differ from his.

Ask your son what he believes makes him a good friend and a good boyfriend. Be attentive and allow him to express his views and beliefs honestly. Create a safety plan for him if he feels like he is in a compromising situation, and include other adults who he feels he can trust if he feels too shy or afraid to come to you.

It is important to let him know that he has options for who to go to when he has questions about friendships, peer pressure, mutual consent, and romantic relationships.

DEBUNKING THE RUMOR MILL:
WHAT SHOULD I DO IF I DON'T LIKE WHO MY SON'S DATING?

Not liking your son's significant other is a dilemma. This is a person who probably has the majority of your son's attention, and that will be hard. It will also be hard for your son as he will feel a sense of tension between you and his romantic partner. It will be hard for you as well because have to watch your son mature and make choices that you might not agree with.

Reflect on the key reasons why you don't like his partner. Do you feel like his partner is being a bad influence or is too distracting? Does this person cop an attitude with you? Or are you jealous because you are losing a part of your connection with your son? Be honest with yourself. This is an important element for you to reflect on. These are some questions you want to ask yourself:

→ Am I ready to watch my teen son enter the dating scene?

→ Do I genuinely believe my son is mature enough to date?

→ Do I have any physical or emotional safety concerns for him in this relationship?

→ Do I believe his partner is negatively influencing him and in what way?

→ Have I set dating boundaries and expectations with him?

continued >>

Your son will want to continue to date the partner of his choice, and history has shown that teens will almost always go against their parents' wishes when it comes to a relationship that their parents don't approve of. It is forbidden therefore it becomes even more attractive. Once you have identified the reasons why you don't like your son's partnership, it will allow for a more streamlined and factual conversation with your child. Have an open and frank conversation with your son. Let him know that you respect his choices but also want to voice your opinion. Set boundaries, rules, and curfews.

Discuss teen dating violence and red flags with your son in a very general way. This will allow for him to make connections to the behaviors and elements that are part of his relationship. The parent-child conversations help your son create a more satisfactory relationship with his girlfriend or boyfriend. Identify what teen violence, manipulation, mental health issues, sexual harassment, respecting boundaries, and healthy communication look like for your teen. Take his ideas, views, and thoughts into consideration and engage in conversation about these topics with him. This will allow for him to feel seen and heard and also establish the importance of expressing his needs in an assertive and healthy fashion.

STUDY PREP: YOUR POSITIVE PARENTING NOTES

Five easy ways to incorporate positive parenting in your household in relation to your son's social life include the following:

1. **Present a united front.** All homes have different family compositions. If you are a two-parent home or in a co-parenting situation, it is important to present a united front with your son. This will allow for clarity and prevents your son from manipulating you by playing two sides against each other. If you and your co-parent disagree about something, do not have that conversation in front of your teen. Let it go while in front of your teen and discuss it after in a private conversation.

2. **Discuss acceptable behaviors.** Make sure your teen understands rules and boundaries that are acceptable in your home with regard to dating, going out with friends, engaging in risky behaviors, and sex. Make a list of expectations for him so that you are not struggling to present them right as you have the conversation. Be prepared to listen to your son and be willing to amend the rules as he matures and demonstrates his capacity to make safe and healthy decisions for himself.

3. **Get to know his friend group.** The friends your son chooses are a reflection of him. Make sure you are open to getting to know them and why your son is attracted to this particular friend group. Identify any red flags and discuss these with your son. Don't be critical of his friends, but establish what is acceptable in your home. Allow space for your child to build his friendships while also being alert. Discuss peer pressure, bullying, and being able to say no.

4. Continue family meetings. Consistency is key. Spending time with your child continues to be an important part of his development, providing continuity in your parent-child bond. Make these meetings a ritual that is not seen as a chore or punitive. Utilize this time to converse about the things that are happening in your son's life, praising his healthy choices. Have realistic expectations for him based on his developmental stage and the behaviors and choices he has made thus far. Meetings should be positive and collaborative with all members of the family. Get creative, and also encourage your child to help plan these meetings. Ensure that everyone (adults and children) gets a chance to speak and create a respectful environment where all opinions are taken into consideration.

5. Let go. This is probably the hardest of all parenting tips. Learning to gradually let go as your son continues to develop his independence can be challenging. However, this will be crucial as your child continues his transition from adolescence to adulthood. Discuss how and when you are establishing additional responsibilities and privileges for him. This will be an ongoing conversation and it should include him in the conversation. Identify how he is earning trust with you and allow for him to continue to grow in his autonomy. Recognize that he will make mistakes, as they are a healthy part of his teenage journey. He will learn to implement his problem-solving skills and learn from past mistakes. Provide him with a safe space to discuss mistakes and how he can grow from them.

KEY TAKEAWAYS

This chapter emphasized the importance of friendships and romantic relationships for your son's development, autonomy, and voyage into adulthood. Friendships evolve from simply enjoying playtime to sharing similar interests, views, and values. Your son will explore his sexuality, gender identity, and gender orientation. It is important to give him the space and support to do so. You will not like all of your son's friends or partners, and it will be important for you to address that with fairness and tact in order to avoid being ostracized by your son. Set clear boundaries and expectations when it comes to risky behaviors and dating. Make sure your son knows the possible repercussions of his actions as well as consequences in the home setting.

- Provide a safe space for conversation about friendships and romantic relationships. Have open dialogue about what boundaries and respect in all relationships should look like. Discuss values established in your home setting that you want to be a part of his life as he continues into adulthood.

- Discuss the effects of peer pressure, bullying, and risky behaviors to fit in with friends. Create a safety plan for your child should he feel the need to have support from other adults when he is not ready to come to you.

- Create a space for learning and growing by allowing your child to gain more privileges and responsibilities as he matures and gains independence. Incorporate him into the conversation as he evolves in his individuality.

- Continue to have family time and remain consistent. It is important for your child to know you support his autonomy along with a continued bond with you. Create some healthy distance, but remain his refuge at the ready.

CHAPTER 5

DISCUSSING BODY IMAGE & BULLYING WITH TEENAGE BOYS

In this chapter we will address several issues your teen might face in regard to his interactions with peers, body image, and hazing. The differences between roughhousing, sexual assault, hazing, and bullying will also be discussed here. Take note of your son's reactions and behaviors and set firm expectations when it comes to explaining your values and beliefs around bullying and hazing. Risk factors associated with both bullying and hazing include a higher risk of depression and anxiety, plus there is the possibility of legal penalties with hazing.

Body image issues your son might experience will also be reviewed. Weight and comparisons to others play a role in your son's body image and can lead to his engaging in unhealthy eating or exercise habits. He might feel pressures in school, social, and athletic settings. We will also explore how the connection between sports training and his body image can lead to unsafe habits or injuries.

The risks of eating disorders come from the pressure to perform and look a certain way, and understanding the impacts it can have on your son is vital to the safety of your child when he is participating in sports. Brain injury and concussions, as well as their long-term effects, will be addressed in order to create awareness for you and your child's safety and well-being. As in all chapters, this will conclude with the positive parenting techniques you should implement with your child.

WHEN ROUGHHOUSING BECOMES MORE: THE PREVALENCE OF SEXUAL ASSAULT AMONG BOYS

Sexual assault is a scary topic to address, especially when discussing it with your child. However, creating awareness and acquiring knowledge will allow for you to be better prepared to educate your son on the prevention of sexual assault and help him understand that you are a support system for him. The prevalence of sexual assault is more notable in female teens, but male teens also experience some form of sexual assault. According to the National Sexual Violence Resource Center, more than 35 percent of boys have been coerced by an acquaintance into victimizing someone else. It is also important to note that one out of six men has been a victim of sexual assault before the age of 18. This number does not account for the boys and men who have never disclosed their assaults.

Roughhousing is very common among teen boys, as from an early age they are provided with toys and games that encourage aggressive and dominating behaviors—toy guns, action figures, violent video games. This sets a standard that is encompassed in the toxic masculinity mindset of being "tough," "stronger and better," and "manly" to meet traditional gender norms. When teen boys do not feel like they are meeting the standards of "manliness," they are more likely to resort to sexual violence as a form of proving their masculinity to their peers.

It is important to note that roughhousing is normal in teen boys and can be a healthy outlet. Engaging in roughhousing can be a great way for your son to exert some of his aggression. Aggression and violence are two very different actions, however. Although aggression can be controlled and guided, it is important to note that violence is dangerous and requires immediate intervention.

Later on in this chapter we will also discuss how hazing and locker room environments contribute to sexual assault among teen peers. Have a conversation with your child about the importance of exerting his aggression but also setting boundaries for his body and respecting the privacy and safety of his peers. Discuss peer pressure, bullying, the need to fit in, and keeping safe and out of harm's way. Remind your son that you are a support system that will help him in any situation that may arise.

Have a conversation about sexual assault and create a safe space that invites him to ask questions and express his opinions, views, and concerns. Discuss how sexual assault occurs when a person is forced, coerced, or manipulated into any unwanted sexual activity. If your child is dismissive of this conversation, remind him of its importance and the concerns that you might have for his safety.

IS HE BEING BULLIED OR IS *HE* THE BULLY?

Bullying is defined as aggressive or unwanted behavior that gives a perceived imbalance of power and is repetitive. During his adolescence, your child will have some type of interaction with bullying, whether as the person engaging in bullying others, the person being bullied, a witness, a defender, or a contributor to this type of behavior. Bullying can take form in physical, social, and verbal ways, and it can be overt or insidious. It can occur in school, social, and cyber settings. Whether your child is being bullied, engaging in bullying others, or has another role in the bullying behavior, it can have lasting effects on his psyche. Foster knowledge in your home and discuss with your son the issues and effects of bullying. Be aware of his behaviors and interactions with his peers. If your child is being bullied, he might be fearful of reporting it or coming to you for support for fear of how the bully may respond, including any threats he may receive if he says anything.

Some of the signs of being bullied can include unexplained bruises, missing items or money, sleep issues or nightmares, changes in mood or appetite, and poor school grades and attendance. The effects of bullying on your child can also include mental health difficulties, including depression, anxiety, and hopelessness. Have an open line of communication with your son and encourage him to set boundaries with others and come to you with any concerns of bullying he may be encountering. If you have concerns that he is at risk for being bullied, lead him in practicing assertive communication to set boundaries with his peers.

If your child is engaging in the bullying, you might see frequent detention or calls to the principal's office, aggressive behaviors, or unexplained items and money. Perhaps your son is having a hard time taking responsibility for his actions and is concerned about his reputation. If you suspect your child is engaging in bullying a peer, confront him. Inquire as to what is leading to these choices and where he has learned this behavior. Remind him of your values, beliefs, rules, and expectations he has as your son and how bullying is unacceptable and comes with consequences. For any child who is having an adverse response to bullying, offer support through mental health therapy or online resources (see Resources at the end of this book).

DEBUNKING THE RUMOR MILL:
I'VE HEARD THAT HAZING HAPPENS TO A LOT OF FRESHMAN BOYS ON SPORTS TEAMS. IS THAT TRUE?

Hazing is a scary thought to have when your child decides to join a sports team. Teens have a sense of secrecy when it comes to hazing, therefore numbers do not necessarily accurately represent what and how often this might be happening. Based on reports, it is estimated that 1.5 million students are hazed annually, and of those 25 percent are under the age of 13. Twenty-four percent of high school athletes reported having been hazed, with male students being more likely than girls to be involved in hazing.

It is important to note that hazing has several categorizations, including intimidation, harassment, and violence. Intimidation has the lowest likelihood of being recognized but the highest likelihood of frequency. Violence on the other hand has the highest likelihood of recognition but occurs less frequently when compared to intimidation and harassment. Examples of intimidation include deception, assigning demerits, demeaning names, socially isolating new teammates, and demands of silence for long periods with implied threats for violations. Harassment includes verbal abuse, threats or implied threats, sleep deprivation, ordering one to wear embarrassing attire, and sexual simulations. Violence can involve forced consumption of drugs or alcohol, water intoxication, abduction or kidnapping, and sexual assault.

Oftentimes hazing starts off with the benevolent intention of creating a bond between teammates and can go too far and cause serious physical or emotional harm. Although hazing has a higher percentage of occurrence on

continued >>

sports teams (24 percent), it is not the sole situation where it occurs. According to statistical data, hazing occurs in peer groups or gangs (16 percent), music, art, or theater groups (8 percent), and even church groups (7 percent). Although there is no data that divides hazing percentages based on grade level, it is important to note that it generally happens as a rite of initiation when teens are entering or becoming part of the team or group. This usually puts the younger and newer teammates at greater risk of being hazed.

Make sure you are having a conversation with your child about hazing. This can loop into your discussion about bullying, and you can help your son sort through the similarities and differences. Remind him that he has the right to feel safe and not be hurt physically or emotionally. Talk about the dangers of hazing as well as the possible legal implications for those who take part in hazing. It is important to remind your child that you and adults in the school setting want to support him and keep him safe.

NEGATIVE BODY IMAGE IMPACTS BOYS ON & OFF THE COURT

Your teen son's physical appearance becomes more important to him during adolescence, particularly in high school. This is when he is becoming increasingly aware of the changes in his body and comparing himself to other peers. Body image is the way he perceives his own physique and how he thinks others see it. Television, social media, peers, and societal expectations affect body image, including issues such as dissatisfaction. Although it is more common for female teens to struggle with body image issues it is important to note that 25 percent of those afflicted by eating disorders are male teens.

If your son is challenged with issues related to his weight or body type, this can lead him to engage in eating disorder behaviors such as abstaining from certain foods, limiting his caloric intake, binge eating, or purging. Eating disorders have many potential triggers, including family issues, low self-esteem, psychological issues, pressure to perform on a sports team, or even genetics. Although there is a lot of information available about the signs of an eating disorder, it is harder to identify in men. Some behaviors to be aware of include changes to your child's eating habits, weight or appetite fluctuations, increase or changes in exercise routine, a difference in skin and hair condition, and excessive use of the bathroom particularly during or immediately after meals. If you are concerned that your son might have an eating disorder, seek professional support immediately in order to prevent further psychological and physical harm.

Sports can add an extra component of pressure to body image issues that lead to disordered eating. The locker room is full of competition, pressure, and banter over who the strongest, most fit, and best athletes are. Sports that have been found to contribute most to disordered eating are gymnastics, bodybuilding, dance, swimming, wrestling, crew, and running. These sports create a higher risk for eating disorders as they are scored for individual success as opposed to sports that focus on team performance, such as basketball, football, and soccer.

For teens looking to "bulk up" or get six-pack abs, overconsumption of protein supplements and other performance-enhancement products might lead to steroid use. In team sports, body dysmorphia and, more specifically, muscle dysmorphia can lead your son to engage in some unhealthy patterns of behavior. Practice and training can take a turn for the worse if your son feels like he needs to catch up to his peers as he might overexert himself and cause physical damage.

Participating in sports might lead to depression and feelings of low self-esteem as well as bullying and hazing that might be taking place in the locker room. Sports, of course, also offer benefits for your son. This is not intended to scare you away from allowing him to participate in sports. Rather it is to create awareness as to some of the risks as your son engages in organized physical activities.

STRENGTH TRAINING IS MORE THAN WEIGHT LIFTING

Strength can be defined in many different aspects of a person's life and goes beyond the physical components. If your teen is participating in weight lifting for the purpose of competition, increasing self-esteem, or improving self-care, have a conversation with him about what *strength* means to him. Discuss also the importance of the mental and emotional strength that are necessary in strength training.

It is also good that when discussing *strength training*, inspire your son to determine what that entails for him. With strength training, the emphasis should be placed on building stamina, creating balance, and allowing rest for his body. Nemours KidsHealth describes strength training as a way to "improve overall fitness; increase lean body mass (more muscle, less fat); burn more calories; make bones stronger; and improve mental health."

Strength training provides your son an opportunity to focus on a goal and the ability to see and reap the benefits of his commitment and consistency. This could create a very fine line for him to balance between training hard and training safely, as the pressures to meet certain standards is high during adolescence. Incorporate this into your conversation and make it an open discussion in regard to his intent behind building up his strength and muscle mass. Have a conversation about what he feels are the benefits of weight lifting and inquire about safety measures he takes to ensure he doesn't get injured.

Discussing mental health and the benefits of strength training is important. Some of the mental health benefits that come through strength training can include a decrease in depressive and anxious symptoms and an increase in self-esteem and self-worth. Although there are a lot of benefits with proper strength training, pressure to perform can result in your son engaging in unhealthy habits or setting unrealistic expectations for himself that can lessen self-worth, self-esteem, and mood.

Participate in your son's weight lifting and strength training plan. Have a conversation with him based on what he hopes to achieve. It is also a good idea to meet with his coach or trainer in order to form an understanding of what the reasonable goals and expectations of your son's strength training entail. Encourage your son to train steadily and at a healthy, steady pace in order to achieve his goals and not push himself. This is a great time to remind him of patience when working toward a goal.

DEBUNKING THE RUMOR MILL: IS IT TRUE THAT BOYS WHO GET SPORTS-RELATED CONCUSSIONS CAN HAVE SEVERE PERSONALITY SHIFTS?

Concussions are considered traumatic brain injuries (TBI) and, according to the Centers for Disease Control and Prevention (CDC), are "caused by a bump, blow, or jolt to the head or by a hit to the body that causes the head and brain to move rapidly back and forth. This sudden movement can cause the brain to bounce around or twist in the skull, creating chemical changes in the brain and sometimes stretching and damaging brain cells."

Although concussions are typically deemed a mild form of TBI and not typically life-threatening, they can have long-lasting effects. Research shows concussions affect children and adolescents differently than adults. Although the brain damage from concussions is less severe

continued >>

in children than for adults, the changes on the brain outlast the symptoms. Some symptoms your child might experience after a concussion include decreased reaction times, memory and concentration problems, irritability, insomnia, and fatigue.

Some studies suggest that children and adolescents being cleared to return to activities once symptoms have decreased don't necessarily receive sufficient time for the brain to heal and to prevent further harm through a second sports-related injury. Second-impact syndrome is when symptoms from a first concussion are still present, causing rapid swelling of the brain after a second concussion. The CDC has created HEADS Up to Youth Sports, a free online training program to educate parents, coaches, and athletes about concussion safety.

Several factors can lead to behavioral changes in a child who has suffered a concussion. Studies show that some effects of a concussion can last for many years after the injury. The severity of the concussion, the amount of time someone took off to heal, and secondary concussions are all additional risk factors for longer-lasting effects, including attention and motor problems, which can manifest depression, anxiety, angry outbursts, and other personality shifts due to some of the difficulties the child is now experiencing in his executive functioning.

Symptomatic recovery of a concussion can occur at around 21 days, and it's important to be mindful of any other changes that are occurring in your son's behavior, alertness, and concentration. For some adolescents, recovery time can last with some symptoms still present for up to 90 days. If you have concerns about your son's recovery or personality changes from a concussion, seek medical attention and don't ignore the symptomology.

STUDY PREP: YOUR POSITIVE PARENTING NOTES

Five easy ways to incorporate positive parenting in your household in regard to body image or bullying include the following:

1. Don't tell him what to do. It is important to allow him a certain amount of autonomy and also include him in decision-making when setting boundaries and expectations. For example, if your son is concerned with his appearance, allow him to make decisions about it while still holding him accountable to the boundaries set in your home.

2. Develop common interests with your son. This will allow for you and your son to have a better relationship and also promote an easier flow of conversation. Don't turn this into a chore for him or set pressures that take away from the fun. For example, if you bond over a sport, don't push him to be the best and don't put him down for not meeting your expectations. Just have fun! This is meant to bring you together and to have memorable experiences. While you are forming a bond, you are also creating an awareness of who your child is surrounding himself with and what his interests are. You will likely be more aware if he begins engaging in behaviors that lead to bullying or are a response to being bullied.

3. Build structure. Structure and consistency are important components for your teen's security and growth. Set expectations for structure and family time, such as weekly family nights or dinners with no phones at the table. Include your son in the development of family time so that it meets his needs and schedule as well. Create a space for everyone to share and catch up on what's going on in their individual lives. When you build strong connections and consistency

in your home setting, it will also allow for you to develop awareness of any behavioral changes your son may be experiencing in response to bullying or body image issues.

4. Be available. You are setting up your standard of being available when your son needs you. Make sure he is aware of your schedule and his importance in it. If you tell your son that you are available for him, then make sure you follow through when he reaches out. Make the time for him if he calls you—even if it's just a few minutes. Don't be dismissive of him or too busy. Reaching out and asking for help is difficult. If your son approaches you with an issue, assess the situation and validate him. Praise him for seeking your support and ask him how you can help. This is a crucial time in your relationship with your son, so continue to establish solid trust as he lets himself be vulnerable with you.

5. Teach and encourage the value of diversity. Establish what diversity means in your home as well as the expectations that are set forth for your son. This is an important component of your teen's development and will inspire him to grow in inclusiveness. This will also help decrease aggressive or bully-type behaviors with peers. Set firm expectations, pointing out examples of what this looks like to your teen. Remind your son that you do not allow intolerant comments or behaviors in your home, and emphasize the importance of acceptance of all people, especially embracing those who have differing religious, cultural, ethnic, financial, sexual, or gender identities.

KEY TAKEAWAYS

In this chapter you have learned about body image, including the perception your child has of himself and how he thinks others perceive him. Take time to talk with your son about his views as well as the expectations he has of himself. Allow him to express himself without judgment—even if you don't agree—and honor his feelings. Provide support in an empathetic and kind manner. Have open and frank conversations with him over body image, self-esteem, self-love, and peer pressure. Inquire as to what he needs from you to feel safe to come to you when a difficult situation arises.

- Discuss the differences between roughhousing and playful behavior and how that is different from assault. Have open dialogue about sexual assault as well. Teach your son to respect others' bodies and choices, as well as the importance of setting appropriate boundaries when others approach your son in a verbal or physical way that does not feel comfortable to him. Although this might be uncomfortable for you and your son, it is important to address this topic with him in order to open the avenues of communication and allow space for him so he feels safe coming to you with questions.

- Be direct about bullying. Bullying is not okay. Make it simple and straightforward. Explain the possible repercussions of engaging in bullying. Set firm expectations about respecting a no-bullying policy in your home—including hazing. Have a conversation with him also about being bullied and remind him of your love and support with either situation. Let him know it is important to seek help from you or a trusted adult if he feels he is being bullied.

- Know that body image matters to your son. Let him know you are supportive of him and be aware of his views of himself. Be mindful of his eating and workout habits. Discuss healthy eating and workout options with him. If he is part of a sports team, make sure you are aware of the expectations set forth for him and that you agree with the plan set for him by his coach.

CHAPTER 6

TEACHING SEX ED TO TEENAGE BOYS

In this chapter we will discuss the importance of educating your son on the topic of sex—even when neither of you feels he's quite ready to engage in sex yet. Still, it is important to start having these conversations with your son as early as junior high or middle school, as this is when kids will start to develop romantic or sexual interests among peers. Having a conversation about sex and all it entails will ensure that your son receives factual information and learns about it from an adult who cares about him. Making the topic of sex taboo will leave him resorting to assumptions and following peer advice, which can turn into unhealthy decisions or engaging in risky behaviors, such as "learning" from pornography.

Related topics addressed in this chapter include consent, accessibility to contraceptives, and the responsibility that comes with engaging in sexual activity.

Discussing sex with your teen is healthy and will help him develop a healthy relationship with sex and to set boundaries that feel comfortable to him. During this time, you can encourage your child to explore his sexual and gender identity while providing a safe and educational space for him to grow and learn.

Enthusiastic consent is a crucial part of engaging in sexual activity, so explaining this to your son is fundamental to his awareness and responsibility when it comes to participating in healthy sexual actions. It's ideal to have several conversations about sex, setting your boundaries and expectations of him.

Although it might seem scary to open the door to the topic of sex, it is a vital part of his life as he transitions into adulthood and explores healthy sexual experiences and relationships.

WHY YOU SHOULD TALK TO YOUR TEEN ABOUT SEX (EVEN IF YOU DON'T WANT THEM TO HAVE IT)

Yes, let's talk about S-E-X! Sex is normal and healthy, so it is important to have open dialogue with your son about it no matter how uncomfortable it feels for either of you. According to the CDC, more than half of teens have had sex by the age of 18. Therefore, having this conversation with your son early on and then continuing with discussions throughout the years will inspire him to engage in sex responsibly.

As awkward as it might seem at first, this is a great time to discuss the different forms of sexual contact, such as masturbation, kissing, heavy petting, dry humping, fingering, hand jobs, oral sex, anal sex, and sexual intercourse. Sexually transmitted diseases (STDs) and pregnancy are also very important topics to address. This is a great time to also discuss consent, peer pressure, safe sex, and contraceptives.

Recognize that your son will engage in masturbation at a young age. Normalize masturbation, as this is a feel-good activity for him long before it becomes sexually driven. It is important to set boundaries that masturbation should only be engaged in private and never in front of others. Conversely, be respectful of his privacy, knocking before entering his bedroom or the bathroom. This is how your son learns about and explores his body, and many children—both male and female—engage in masturbation as young as when they are toddlers.

As your son grows into adolescence, he will also begin to experiment sexually and develop romantic attractions. Your son will engage in romantic and sexual relationships as early as junior high or middle school, and the likelihood of sexual activity increases with each year that passes. Although this might seem unnerving, it is important to create awareness and address sex as your son continues to mature and begins to engage in sexual activity. Recognize and accept that your child might engage in sexual activity at a younger age and stage of development than you'd anticipated. This is why it is essential to start having this open dialogue with him and create a space where sex can be discussed openly early on.

Talk to him about peer pressure and consent, as well as taking the time he needs before he engages in any sexual activity that he doesn't feel ready to participate in. Remind him that consent isn't just about his partner consenting. It is also about his consent and feeling ready and comfortable to engage in the sexual activity. Discuss contraception and safe-sex options and their proper applications, but STDs and pregnancy should not be utilized as scare tactics—rather, educate and inform your son of some of the possible ramifications of engaging in sexual activity so he grasps the importance of engaging in safe sex.

This will be an ongoing conversation and should be based on your son's emotional awareness and curiosity. Discussing sex with him will create a space for him to ask questions about things that may concern him. You can also provide him with reputable resources he can use if he feels uncomfortable talking to you about sex.

ENTHUSIASTIC CONSENT IS KEY

It is imperative to teach your son about touch and consent in his relationships. Identifying healthy boundaries is a vital component of establishing enthusiastic consent. Allow for your son to have a part in this conversation, and discuss the differences between consent, peer pressure, and coercion. Remind him that it is necessary to discuss consent with his partner and consider each other's needs when engaging in any form of sexual activity. This includes something as seemingly small as kissing. Talk with him about the significance of never engaging in sexual behavior if he feels pressured by a partner or just wants to fit in.

Enthusiastic consent is defined as a definitive *yes* that can be expressed in various ways either verbally or with physical cues. Consent requires communication with a sexual partner, and it is more than just a passive agreement. Enthusiastic consent means both parties are excited with being part of the decision to engage in sexual activity with each other. Although physical cues might also indicate enthusiastic consent, it is critical to note that a verbal enthusiastic *yes* must be included.

A *yes* can be coerced or lack enthusiasm if the person feels pressured or is under the influence of drugs or alcohol. Having sex with someone who delivers a less-than-enthusiastic *yes* or a *yes* while under the influence of drugs or alcohol is considered sexual assault. Coercion, which is convincing or being convinced to participate in a sexual activity that is not desired, is also considered assault. When discussing consent with your son, this will be a key point to discuss with him. Both he and his partner should engage in sexual activity only when both give enthusiastic consent. It will also be important to address legal penalties when it comes to consent and sexual assault. Remind your son that it is important to set healthy and clear boundaries for himself and also to honor his partner's boundaries.

DEBUNKING THE RUMOR MILL: I'VE HEARD THAT TALKING TO YOUR TEEN ABOUT SEX WILL MAKE THEM THINK IT'S OKAY TO HAVE IT RIGHT AWAY. IS THAT TRUE?

Discussing sex and all that comes with it is not the same as saying you are okay with your son having sex. It will be important for you to express your concerns simply and honestly when it comes to him having sexual contact with someone else. You can incorporate your views on sexual contact as well as your expectations for his engagement in sexual activity during this time. While opening the avenues of communication with him about sex, you can also feel free to share your opinion concerning when you think it is appropriate for him to have sex based on your values and beliefs.

It is also important to recognize that he has his own views and ideas about how and when he wants to explore his sexuality with a partner. Allowing him to have a safe and nonjudgmental space to express his wants, needs, and questions will be vital to keeping the lines of communication between you open. Recognize that it is also normal for your son to explore his sexual identity and preferences. Starting these conversations early with your son can bring about a foundation for having a healthy and positive relationship with sex for him and allow for him to explore his wants, needs, and desires while maintaining healthy boundaries and expectations for himself.

Talking casually about sex lets your child to normalize it as part of his adolescence and adulthood while providing the knowledge for him to mature into his sexuality. Some

continued >>

of the benefits of having these conversations with your child include awareness of his body, body positivity, gender identity, identification of healthy boundaries, knowledge of enthusiastic consent, and recognizing sexual assault or abuse.

Engaging in these conversations may feel awkward at first, but it is a good idea to have multiple conversations about this topic over time so as to not overwhelm your teen or yourself. The conversations will develop in complexity over time as your son grows into his sexuality. But, no, being a sex-positive parent does not mean you are giving permission or encouragement for your son to engage in sex. It just means you are preparing him and creating awareness for sex to be a positive and healthy part of his life.

As he is establishing his identity and sense of self, these conversations will also allow for him to have awareness of his body and help him differentiate between healthy and unhealthy sexual patterns. It also offers opportunities for you to have a conversation with him about his sexual orientation and gender identity, as well as develop fluidity in conversation so that he feels comfortable discussing his feelings and emotions with you.

WHERE TRADITIONAL SEX ED FALLS SHORT

Traditional sex education has been a part of the educational system for a long time and ranges in the amount of information it provides depending on grade level, as well as the district, county, or state where the students attend school. In some states, you as a parent or guardian must consent for your child to study sex ed in school—there are no federal mandates at this time regarding sex ed.

The Sexuality Information and Education Council of the United States (SIECUS), a sex ed advocacy initiative, has created a guideline for students in the classroom ranging from kindergarten through 12th grade in an effort to have a nationwide standard when it comes to creating knowledge and awareness of sex education. SIECUS recommends six key concepts for inclusion in sex education: 1) human development, 2) relationships, 3) personal skills, 4) sexual behavior, 5) sexual health, and 6) society and culture. Although a curriculum is readily available and used in many schools, it is not a requirement by law to be utilized in school curricula across the nation.

Sex education can also vary depending on whether your son attends public, private, or parochial school. It is important to note that although sex education is taught in school settings, it is merely a one-day class in junior high and high school as opposed to an ongoing conversation and course about sexual education. Arguably, sex is a complex subject with a range of subtopics that require more than one day to cover comprehensively. Although it is normal for your son to learn some sex education from his peers, a more formal education might be in order for your child to gain a better understanding of sex.

Identify areas that you feel are important for your son to know about. Based on your family's values, beliefs, cultural factors, and your son's gender and sexual orientation, you can have an ongoing conversation with him about sex. Create a plan to address his specific choices and needs as well as your expectations for him. SIECUS has a free downloadable PDF titled *National Sex Education Standards: Core Content and Skills, K–12* with guidelines to help you and educators teach your child about sex in an age-appropriate manner. Utilize reputable, factual, and scientific resources when teaching your child about sex.

Some topics you might want to address with your son can include the anatomy of the vagina and penis, STDs (including HIV and AIDS), types of contraceptives and responsible use of them, pregnancy and options if pregnancy occurs (keeping the baby, adoption, abortion, the mother's rights to choose). Additionally, peer pressure to engage in sex, debunking common myths, sexual orientation, and gender identity should also be incorporated into your conversations about sex. If you don't have the answers for some of your son's questions, be honest with him and include him in the learning process as you locate reputable sources for answers and solutions. This is a great opportunity to model utilizing reliable and scientific research for him.

IT'S IMPORTANT TO TALK ABOUT NON-HETEROSEXUAL SEX (EVEN IF YOU THINK YOUR TEEN IS STRAIGHT)

As we continue to discuss sex and your son's exploration of self, it is essential to note it can also include gender identity and sexual orientation. Love, acceptance, and open communication are vital. Whether your teen is straight or identifies as LGBTQIA+ (lesbian, gay, bisexual, transgender, queer, intersex, asexual, plus other gender identities), it is important to discuss sexuality, gender identity, and pronouns with him. This will help him recognize and explore inclusivity as well as indicate that his home is a safe place for him to discuss his views, beliefs, and choices.

As a parent, it is important to have awareness of sexual orientation, gender identity, and pronoun use. *Sexual orientation* refers to what gender or genders a person is romantically or sexually attracted to, and it includes heterosexual, gay, bisexual, pansexual, and asexual. *Gender identity* is a person's own identification of gender and incorporates the sex that's assigned at birth—for example, a person who is assigned male at birth who identifies as male, a person who is assigned male at birth who identifies as female, or a nonbinary person who identifies as both male and female or neither or outside of the gender binary. *Pronoun use* is how a person is identified based on their gender identity and includes she/her, he/him, ze/hir, and singular they/them. Some people will have a preference for more than one pronoun, such as a teen who identifies as he/him and also they/them.

Whether your son identifies as heterosexual or part of the LGBTQIA+ community, it is important to have this conversation in order to let your son know that you are an inclusive home and open to his exploration of his sexuality and gender identification. As discussed previously, adolescence is the time for your son to learn who he is and what he likes, including his romantic and sexual interests, as well as his sexuality, gender identity, and pre-ferred pronouns. Discuss your family values and beliefs, and listen to your son and validate his feelings as well. This is a great time to reflect on toxic masculinity and how that might play a role in your son's choices.

Prior to this conversation, honestly process how you feel about your son's potential sexual orientation. Create a welcoming space in navigating what same-sex and gender-fluid sex looks like for your son.

DEBUNKING THE RUMOR MILL:
CAN SCHOOLS ENFORCE ABSTINENCE-ONLY SEX ED CLASSES?

Depending on where you reside, your local school's state, county, or district determines what is taught in your son's sex ed class—that is, if your son's school even teaches sex ed. It is important to note that presently only 30 of the 50 states in the United States have laws that require sex education be taught in schools. However, there is no guarantee of what type of course material is being taught due to the lack of regulations. LGBTQIA+ inclusive ter-minology and education are also left to state and local government discretion.

continued >>

From 1982 to 2010, the United States government has spent more than two billion dollars on abstinence-only-until-marriage sex education programs. Presently, 19 states adhere to standards that teach abstinence-only sex education, which is also known as Sexual Risk Avoidance Education (SRAE). In this form of sex education, information about contraception, pregnancy, and STDs is not provided, as the expectation is that teens abstain from sexual contact. Teenagers are in an exploratory phase and will more than likely engage in some form of sexual interaction at some stage of their adolescence.

The following states currently follow the SRAE model: Arizona, Arkansas, Florida, Georgia, Indiana, Kentucky, Louisiana, Michigan, Minnesota, Mississippi, Missouri, Montana, North Dakota, Ohio, Oklahoma, Tennessee, Texas, Utah, and Wisconsin. Additionally, there are also some states that incorporate an abstinence-plus sex ed program that encourages abstinence but also incorporates information about condoms and other forms of contraception.

The biggest concern with abstinence-only programs lies in the lack of knowledge that can leave your son with minimal information when he is deciding to engage in sexual activity. This is where your input becomes crucial and necessary to your son's sexual awareness and responsibility when deciding to engage in sexual activity. It will also minimize the likelihood of his engaging in unsafe or risky sexual activity with very little resources or knowledge.

Also concerning is that abstinence-only education is not inclusive of the LGBTQIA+ community, leaving some students to feel ostracized or feeling like they have to hide their sexual orientation or identity. This can lead to issues with self-esteem and negative mental health impacts for teens. Research indicates that the abstinence-only approach does not prevent teens from engaging in sexual activity and ultimately leaves youth ill-equipped when it comes to contraceptive use and preventing teen pregnancy.

STUDY PREP: YOUR POSITIVE PARENTING NOTES

Five easy ways to incorporate positive parenting in educating your teen about sex include the following:

1. Do not fake knowledge. If you don't know the answer or solution to a question or issue, it's okay to let your son know that. This will model for him that you are also continuing to learn and grow even in adulthood. This makes you more approachable and sets up a bonding experience for both of you to grow and learn together. By the same token, allow your son to teach you about something he has more knowledge of, such as today's gender-variant and gender-neutral trends. This can also give his self-esteem and self-worth a booster shot as a contributing member of the family. It will also allow for him to recognize that this gives him a voice and that what he has to say and contribute matters. It will show him you are interested in what he has to say.

2. Support your son's maturity. This includes allowing him to take part in conversations in regard to the responsibilities and privileges he continues to gain as he gets older. Support his sexual maturity by praising and acknowledging good decision-making. Be present at school functions and be a support with sex ed homework or assignments. Play an active role in his continued autonomy and independence, giving him the privacy he craves during

adolescence. Allow him to have more social interactions to grow his romantic and sexual relationships. Let him know you are on his team and are rooting for his continued growth and evolvement into adulthood.

3. Recognize mistakes as healthy for growth. Allow him to practice independence by giving him the space to learn and make mistakes. Let him use his problem-solving skills in order to navigate through situations on his own, but remain a source of support if he reaches out for advice. This will allow your son to experiment with task completion as he navigates ways to resolve situations on his own. Be a supporting parent and let him know you are available to support him if he needs it. Stay away from micromanaging, hovering, or pestering him, especially about his personal relationships or sexual orientation. Allow him to embrace his unique and authentic self.

4. Create open dialogue and communication. Some topics are uncomfortable to discuss, and your son will naturally want to stray away from addressing them with you. Even if it makes you squirm, address uncomfortable topics such as sexual activity, sexual orientation, gender identity, and gender pronouns—and honor his choices. Make sure your son knows that you are there for him and willing to engage in these conversations in a judgment-free space to allow for his comfort to grow when reaching out to you with questions or concerns. Continue to have open communication about sexual activity and practicing safe sex. This does not mean you consent to his having sex, but it does mean you want him to make healthy decisions if he chooses to engage in sex.

5. Set age-appropriate expectations. This will help you not partake in an unhealthy cycle of unrealistic expectations that will set your son up for failure. Identify expectations you have for him and determine if they are

developmentally appropriate based on his current age, level of maturity, and stage of development. Continue to have conversations about sex to evolve along with your son's maturing sexuality.

KEY TAKEAWAYS

In this chapter you have learned about sex education and its significance in your son's adolescence. We have explored the importance of open communication and education in your home setting when it comes to creating awareness and knowledge about sex and sexual activity for your son. Discuss sex openly with your son and normalize sexual activity for him as well as instilling the values, beliefs, and expectations you have around sexual activity. Set clear guidelines and provide a welcoming environment for him to come to you with questions or concerns, and do not make it weird or judgmental.

* Sex education is important in school and home settings. Recognize your son might not get a comprehensive sex education program in school, so what he learns at home is vital to his growth and engagement in a healthy sexual relationship with potential partners in adolescence and into adulthood. Make a list of topics to cover, including female and male anatomy, different types of sexual activity, contraceptive options, STDs such as HIV/AIDS, teen pregnancy, enthusiastic consent, healthy communication, and forming romantic relationships.

* Sexual orientation, gender identity, and pronouns are important to address and incorporate into your vocabulary and conversations with your son. Ask him about his preferred gender pronouns, and let him know he is safe to express to you his sexual orientation and gender identity. If you are unsure how to support him, ask him what he needs from you.

- Enthusiastic consent is important. Review with your son the important concept of enthusiastic consent in sexual encounters. Make sure he understands his comfort level and respects others' boundaries as well. Differentiate enthusiastic consent from coercion, and discuss the problematic nature of consent that is given under the influence of alcohol or drugs.

- Healthy boundaries and communication are musts when engaging in sexual activity. Create a safety plan for your son so he can safely contact you or someone else in the event he finds himself in a dangerous situation.

CHAPTER 7

THE SELF-EXPRESSION OF TEENAGE BOYS

Throughout this chapter, we will address some of the ways your teen son is discovering his likes, dislikes, and interests in an effort to identify and express his sense of self. Teens are seeking individuality and autonomy from their parents as they journey through adolescence into adulthood. During this time, he is undergoing many changes and some may be bigger and more impactful than others. Your son will discover his self-identity and explore his preferences by trying different hairstyles, fashion choices, activities, and interests.

The differences between gender fluidity, gender identification, and sexual orientation will also be clarified in this chapter. It is important to note that your son's engaging in activities and behaviors that are traditionally seen as feminine does not necessarily mean he identifies as a member of the LGBTQIA+ community.

In addition, this chapter explores how mental health might be impacted not by his identity choices but by possible backlash, rejection, and bullying he may experience due to being gender nonconforming. Straying from gender stereotypes has become more normalized and accepted, yet it can still garner negative reactions from peers, society, and family, which can result in an increased risk for depression and anxiety.

Goth and punk subcultures will also be explored in this chapter, and we will delve into how this type of music interest is often about more than just the lyrics and melodies—these are communities that express themselves through nontraditional clothing, harsh makeup, and alternative interests that deviate from conformity. These subcultures provide ways for your child to fully express himself. We will also discuss musical choices that are centered on death and your teen's predominantly black wardrobe—are these symptomatic of feeling depressed?

UNDERSTANDING THE (MANY) POTENTIAL COSTUME CHANGES

As we traverse through teenage boys' growth through adolescence, we have learned there is a lot of complexity in their journey into adulthood. Teens will go through a phase of exploration at some point. They are discovering and learning what fits for them as they continue to explore themselves. During this time, they will journey through and explore many different interests and tastes. Some of these may include trying out different looks, fashion styles, interests, activities, friend groups, and other preferences. This is part of their passage into autonomy and figuring out who they are as they become adults.

Your child will make various changes influenced by peers, social media, and television. He is learning who he is and who he wants to be. It can feel confusing for you as a parent, but take solace, for this is a normal part of adolescence. Provide your son with support as he trips through varying interests and experiments with his identity and his preference.

Show interest in his likes and activities. Learn about the music and other activities he may be showing interest in. Find out who he looks up to, and get to know the friends he is surrounding himself with. He is learning to form his identity, and this is an important component of his maturity. Allowing and supporting him as he develops his self-expression will increase his sense of belonging in his adolescence and into his adult years. Determine if there are any factors that make you uncomfortable or that you feel are inappropriate, such as piercings or offensive clothing. Talk with your son about any rules you want to establish, and also the permanent nature of some choices, like tattoos.

As you know, your son is going through physical, social, emotional, and cognitive shifts that can be confusing, exciting, and frustrating for him and you. He is exploring who he is, who he looks up to, and who he wants to become. As his brain continues to develop, this is a peak time for him to learn new things, and he can be a fast learner—if the subject matter interests him. Trying new activities makes him feel good, especially when he picks up something that he is truly interested in and passionate about. He may pick up new interests, including a new music genre, joining a different sports team, or taking up a unique hobby. Any of the activities and interests he engages in serve as building blocks for his burgeoning independence.

Something as simple as changing his hairstyle or accessories can have a huge impact on your son's self-esteem, well-being, and sense of autonomy. For him, this is a lot more than just fashion and hair—it is about independent decision-making and developing his own style personality. How many fashion don'ts do you remember doing as you look back at your own adolescence? As nostalgic, embarrassing, or funny as it might be in hindsight, those choices were pivotal to your formation of self during that time. Remember that as you grant your son flexibility, patience, and grace as he pilots his own path.

WHEN GENDER NONCONFORMING ENTERS STAGE LEFT

Gender fluidity refers to the way your teen expresses himself, which may be fluid between feminine and masculine normative qualities. For example, your son may be an athlete and the star of the football team but also enjoys wearing nail polish or using makeup. Gender identification refers to how a person identifies and was discussed in chapter 6. It is important to take note of how your son wishes to be identified and to use appropriate pronoun choices, which can include feminine she/her, masculine he/him, gender-neutral ze/hir, and singular they/them. Sexual orientation refers to a person's preference and attraction in romantic partners, also discussed at length in chapter 6.

Gender fluidity is now more acceptable and normalized, particularly among teens and young adults, due to social awareness and support. Some teens are open to the idea of breaking away from gender stereotypes to focus on what feels good as a form of self-expression.

During their formative childhood years, around age two or three, kids learn about their gender identification as boys or girls. Gender is something that young children are aware of, but sexuality does not typically come into play until adolescence. It is not uncommon for children who are gender diverse to refuse to be called "boy" or "girl" even if they are assigned male or female at birth.

Society perhaps finds it more acceptable for a teen boy to engage in gender fluidity if he is considered artistic. But that feeds into a stereotype, as gender fluidity can be prevalent with teen boys who are star athletes, science geeks, motor heads, computer techies, and headbangers—it happens across the board. As we explore gender fluidity, it is important to understand that engaging in gender fluidity does not define your son's sexual orientation. In order to understand gender fluidity, it is important to note the differences in gender fluidity and expression, identification, and sexual orientation.

Be self-aware as you discuss gender fluidity with your son. Ask yourself if there are any cultural, societal, or heteronormative ideologies that may become a speed bump for you in understanding your son's choices, beliefs, and views. Toxic masculinity and outdated views of how a man should present, act, and express himself may also play a factor. Recognize these as possible barriers prior to engaging in conversation with your teen, and consciously choose to support him in his gender identity. Come to terms with the fact that he—she/ze/they—might not fall into the traditionally masculine role that you possibly envisioned for him.

DEBUNKING THE RUMOR MILL:
I HEARD THAT MY SON SOMETIMES WEARS DRESSES AND LETS GIRLS AT SCHOOL PUT MAKEUP ON HIM. DOES THAT MEAN HE'S GAY?

Your son's wearing makeup or dresses to school does not necessarily mean he is gay. The best way to know if your son identifies as a member of the LGBTQIA+ community is to ask him straight up. Please note some teens are not fans of labels and do not want to be placed in a categorical box. Because your teen is exploring himself, his interests, and who he is, he might transition or vacillate in his sexuality and gender preferences as he experiments and becomes more comfortable in his own skin.

It is important to note that your son might also identify as nonbinary. According to the Human Rights Campaign, the largest LGBTQ political lobbying organization in the United States, "Nonbinary people may identify as being both a man and a woman, somewhere in between, or as falling completely outside these categories. While many also identify as transgender, not all nonbinary people do. Nonbinary can also be used as an umbrella term encompassing identities such as agender, bigender, genderqueer, or gender-fluid." Drag personas are men who dress in women's clothing along with extravagant hair and makeup. Although most men who engage in drag identify as gay, it is important to note that is not always the case.

continued >>

Men have used makeup since ancient Egyptian times. It was popular around the 17th century when makeup and wigs were worn onstage during Shakespearian plays. In addition, aristocratic men applied white powder to their faces, pink tints to their cheeks, and rouge on their lips and also wore wigs, and this was seen as a representation of their social status.

Many men in the acting industry are open to the idea of makeup as a way of looking attractive. Cosmetics companies, including high-end brands such as Chanel and Tom Ford, have started makeup lines that are geared toward men. Teen girls learn at a young age that makeup is a way to feel empowered and enhance their natural beauty—and hide blemishes that often come with puberty. Teen boys and men are now embracing cosmetic secrets: a little lipstick to make their lips seem more kissable or some concealer to hide the tired-looking under-eye circles after a late-night cram study session. Although it is a possibility your son is embracing his femininity or gender fluidity, he might simply be trying to cover a zit or feel more comfortable around his crush.

IS IT A MENTAL HEALTH ISSUE?

Your son's experimenting with his identity and sexual fluidity does not raise mental health concerns. What can cause some mental health issues, including anxiety and depression, is the backlash or rejection your son might experience from those who are not so open-minded about deviations from social norms. Be alert to your child's behaviors as he experiments with his identity. Is he wearing clothing that is stereotypically more feminine? Has he purchased any makeup or nail polish? Does he act more secretive around you? Do you think he is changing clothes when not at home for fear of rejection from family members?

Be aware of what depression and anxiety might look like. Be open and respectful of your son's choices and be cautious of any biases that could create a barrier or limit your communication with your son. Have an honest reflective moment with yourself as to how gender biases and stereotypes might impact your ability to be supportive of your son's exploration of his gender identity. Identify what makes you uncomfortable and allow yourself to be vulnerable with your teen son when asking how you can support him. Revisit any skewed views or beliefs and consider being more sensitive to and accepting of people's personal gender decisions.

Ask your son to engage in a conversation with you about his sexual fluidity and how you can be supportive. Ask the tough questions that might feel uncomfortable, and let your son educate you on his preferences. Once again remind yourself that he is learning about who he is and what feels comfortable for him, so having a support system at home is vital to his growth and mental health.

Rejection has a huge impact on anyone, especially teens as they are still building their identity, self-esteem, and self-worth. Although teens might initially feel empowered and free when breaking away from gender standards, that can transition to depression and anxiety due to some of the outside criticism or scrutiny they might experience from doing so. These are factors that can impact your son's mental health.

Take note of any changes in your son's mood or behavior. Is he isolating? Does he seem sad? Is he angry or easily triggered? Engage him in conversation and validate his feelings and mood. Listen to him when he shares with you how he is feeling and what he is experiencing and concerned about. Offer support and seek professional help for him if you feel his mental health is adversely affected. Make sure you acknowledge that he is not doing anything wrong when exploring his gender fluidity and preferences.

FROM GOTHS TO PUNKS: WHY THE ANGSTY AESTHETIC IS SO APPEALING

It's been well established that adolescents are discovering themselves, and this includes their taste in music. Music can become not only about the enjoyment of listening but also a form of personal expression through related fashion choices. Those who identify as goth or punk, for example, belong to a subculture. If your child becomes interested in goth or punk, school yourself in the dynamics of the subculture to provide him with support and avoid assumptions about his feelings.

One thing that makes the aesthetics of each of these subcultures so appealing is that it drastically differs from what is traditional in your son's childhood surroundings. He gets to use his music and dress to express himself in a way that sets him apart from the choices made for him by his parental unit, while also bonding with other like-minded members of his subculture.

The angst-ridden nature of the music might appeal to him because he is experiencing anxiety and perhaps even a tinge of subconscious grief as he mourns the loss of his childhood and moves toward adulthood. Goth and punk both became highly popular in the 1970s and continue to be prevalent subcultures. People who are seen as goth or punk typically choose all-black clothing, black or oxblood nail polish, and makeup application that includes washed-out skin tones accented with dark lip shades and harsh eye shadows. Goths often dye their hair black or deep blue, whereas punks usually go for shaved heads or mohawk-style hair. Clunky combat boots are usually the footwear of choice for both subcultures.

Goth and punk are now seen by some as more mainstream, as the initial shock factor seems to have waned. However, it can still feel alarming to watch your child's style change so drastically, particularly if his moods and mental well-being also seem to be affected. Although it is a form of self-expression, it can serve as a slippery slope to an increased risk of depression and self-harm due to the influence of brooding lyrics. Ascertain whether your son's interest in this subculture is a harmless form of expression or if it is seriously affecting his outlook on life.

Goth is often perceived as finding beauty in darkness. Goth music has a dark, moody vibe and is more introspective, and it can be considered comparative to emo music, a genre that is characterized by its focus on emotional expression. The punk subculture is typically seen as nonconformist and rebellious. Punk music is very different from goth music, as it is more aligned with antiestablishment beliefs and teenage rebellion.

If your child is interested in these or other subcultures, ask him what draws him to them. Listen without judgment, and offer a space for him to express himself openly. Identify if there are boundaries or guidelines that you should be following in your home regarding these subcultures, for example, if your child is dressing offensively or threatening to harm himself.

DEBUNKING THE RUMOR MILL:
MY SON WEARS A LOT OF BLACK AND LISTENS TO MUSIC ABOUT DEATH. IS HE DEPRESSED?

Death metal is an extreme form of heavy metal music, and its death-centric lyrics can be chilling to some parents. Because of the morose subject matter, does listening to death metal translate to clinical depression? The short answer is "not necessarily," but it is very possible that your child is having some sad emotions and, yes, he might be experiencing depression. Although in the '80s and '90s, goth and emo set the standards for dark and depressing music, there are other genres like death metal that produce songs with themes of dying, depression, and suicide.

continued >>

Note that other mainstream musicians have produced depressing songs: Hank Williams ("I'm So Lonesome I Could Cry"), Eminem ("Death Becomes Me"), The Weeknd ("Tears in the Rain"), Drake ("Over My Dead Body"), Kendrick Lamar ("Sing About Me, I'm Dying of Thirst"), Lana del Rey ("Born to Die"), and even Notorious B.I.G ("Suicidal Thoughts") have all had songs related to death, suicide, and dying. Studies have found that music is a powerful tool that impacts our mood and can also be reflective of our emotions. If your child is going through a breakup, for example, you might hear him listening to sad music. If your child is having a hard time in class, being bullied, or having depressive symptoms, one of the indicators of his mood could be the music he is listening to. Whether it's indicative of a sad moment or a more serious mental health concern, take interest in your son's musical choices, and engage him in conversation by posing open-ended questions.

Wearing black can also be part of the way your son expresses himself as belonging to a death metal culture. However, as previously mentioned, this might in and of itself be indicative of experiencing depression. Although studies indicate that clothing can be reflective of mood for girls, the same has not been found for boys. This does not apply to gender-fluid teens and is more in line with stereotypical gender norms. Bottom line, don't make assumptions about your son's mood or depressive state based solely on his musical tastes and fashion choices. Avoid knee-jerk reactions, but be aware of other symptoms and behaviors that, when combined with musical choices and fashion expression, might be indicators of mental health problems.

STUDY PREP: YOUR POSITIVE PARENTING NOTES

Five easy ways to incorporate positive parenting in your household to promote and support self-expression include the following:

1. **Ask before assuming.** Don't assume that your child is happy, excited, sad, depressed, or suicidal. Remember, teens are great at hiding their true feelings and emotions, but are more likely to open up to you if you ask your son directly about his emotional state rather than assume. Assumptions will likely lead to his shutting you out, as he might feel like it's pointless to correct you if you are already drawing conclusions without asking him first. If you have concerns about your son's well-being, engage him in conversation regarding some of the behaviors that are concerning and allow him to express his feelings related to your observations. Come to him from a place of compassion and concern over lecturing.

2. **Bring up the tough topics.** If you don't bring them up, how will he know it is safe to talk about them? Create an environment where the proverbial elephant in the room is addressed, and together work through the discomfort of certain topics. Some topics that likely feel scary for him or you include sexual orientation, sex, contraception, spiritual beliefs, gender identity, pronouns, and political views. Make it a point to let your son know that you encourage freethinking and are genuinely interested in his point of view—even if it might differ from your opinions or beliefs.

3. **Be open to embracing change.** Don't overreact. If your son wants to wear makeup or nail polish, embrace it. Have a conversation with him about why this is important to him.

If there are guidelines you want to set, this is a great time to have that conversation with him: "Yes, you can wear nail polish. But I would like for you to wait until you turn 17 before deciding if you want any piercings." Set limits that meet your family's ideologies while also allowing your son's freedom of expression. Make sure you are clear as to what those boundaries and limitations are before having a conversation with him. Be willing to compromise and show some flexibility as your son is exploring his preferences.

4. Allow your child to express himself and speak without interruption. Even if you disagree or are feeling frustrated, practice and model active listening for him. This is a pivotal component of creating a safe space where he feels validated and heard. This also models the importance of engaging in conversation in which both parties are given time to verbalize their feelings and feel heard.

5. Seek out professional help if needed or requested. If your child asks for mental health services, be supportive and praise him for his willingness to ask for help. If you are unsure how to navigate a situation, do not be afraid to seek outside support or help for yourself. Mental health is important, and depression can have serious ramifications for both your teen and your family. Be open to seeking outside help and make sure your teen feels comfortable with any therapist he is seeing. Make him part of the decision-making process, as he is the one who will be spending the majority of his therapeutic sessions with the clinician.

KEY TAKEAWAYS

In this chapter you have learned about the difference between gender fluidity and sexual orientation. You have also learned the importance of embracing and supporting your son's choices as he continues to explore his likes, feelings, emotions, musical choices, and style as he navigates into adulthood. Teen angst might lead to some unusual or even unsavory musical choices and fashion expressions. Finally, you have also learned how some of these choices might be indicative of your son's involvement in a subculture, which could be harmless self-expression but might also point to depressive disorders.

- Recognize that throughout his adolescence your son will explore many different styles of clothing, hairdos, interests, hobbies, friend groups, and activities. This is a normal part of his growth and exploration of self.

- Create awareness of differences between gender fluidity, gender identity, use of pronouns, and sexual orientation. If you are unsure of the definitions, please review them in this chapter. You can also ask your son to teach you about his views on these topics and the impact they have on his life.

- Don't assume he is gay just because he wears makeup or nail polish. Many boys who identify as straight or hetero-sexual as well as gender fluid will use makeup, nail polish, and other cosmetics. Steer clear from assumptions and ask him about his choices and how they are reflective of who he is as a person.

- His musical choices can be part of his identity, particularly when listening to extreme genres such as goth, punk, or death metal. Remember, he probably resonates with a sense of belonging to a group of like-minded people as he delves into his teenage angst. These styles of music may allow him to feel heard, seen, and a part of something greater. Take an interest in the type of music he listens to. Learn about the artists and what attracts him to this type of music.

CHAPTER 8

TALKING ABOUT DRUGS & ALCOHOL WITH TEENAGE BOYS

In this chapter we will delve into alcohol and drug use as well as its potential effects on your child's development and brain. It is essential to also note the short- and long-term effects that underage drinking can have on teens, families, and the community as a whole. The Centers for Disease Control and Prevention (CDC) notes that underage drinking cost the United States 24 billion dollars in 2010. In addition, it is responsible for more than 3,500 deaths per year. Some parents feel that allowing their sons to consume alcohol in the home setting is safer and can help them make smarter decisions. This is a myth, and we will address some of the civil and criminal liabilities parents can face when allowing underage kids to drink at home.

Drug use and vaping will also be studied, and modern drug culture and the impacts of social media, celebrities, and peers will be reviewed. In addition, we will identify key warning signs to look out for if you have concerns about your son's drug use or vaping. Vaping is rising in popularity, and we will explore the dangers and effects it can have on your son. Vaping has surpassed traditional cigarette use and includes the inhalation of nicotine, marijuana, and hash oil. Due to clever marketing strategies, vaping is very popular among teens and young adults, and can cause long-term and serious effects on your son's brain development as well as his overall health. We will look at the differences between nicotine and marijuana use, as well as why vaping is so appealing to teens. Also, we will explore whether or not to share your past drug history with your son before ending with positive and relevant parenting techniques.

TO DRINK OR NOT TO DRINK IS ALWAYS THE QUESTION

Peer pressure will likely impact your teen on more than a few occasions during adolescence. Peer pressure is a significant factor in underage drinking. It is essential to understand that underage drinking is a major public health concern due to the negative effects it can have on individuals, peers, family, and community members. As we have previously discussed, teens tend to engage in risky behaviors as they transition into adulthood. This includes underage drinking, and research notes that underage drinking can lead to other risky behaviors (e.g., binge drinking, sex with multiple partners, drug use) and a higher likelihood of lower grades (mostly D's and F's). Parties and other large group events can be opportunities for your teen to engage in underage drinking or feel pressured to do so in an effort to fit in. Your son wants to consume alcohol in an effort to be seen as one of the gang or "cool," so if his peers are drinking, he might not want to feel left out. He might also consume alcohol to impress a romantic interest or as a form of bonding with his friends. Alcohol has also been incorporated as part of hazing events—he might not only feel pressured but also forced to consume it.

Alcohol can be appealing to your son for many different reasons. It might be a way to temporarily feel good, reduce stress, or relax. He could also be consuming alcohol to feel older or have a sense of making choices independent of parental restrictions. He might be rebelling, bored, or looking for instant gratification.

Finally, he simply could just be curious about it since he has been exposed to it on social media, television, or around adults in his life who drink alcohol socially or in excess. There are many factors that potentially increase your teen's likelihood of engaging in underage drinking. Peer pressure, risk-taking behaviors, personality characteristics, the act of self-medicating, wanting an escape from their problems, savvy marketing, and genetics can influence a teen into consuming alcohol.

As your son learns to problem solve, he might find alcohol is an easy solution to erasing or temporarily forgetting some of the issues he might be facing. If your son starts consuming alcohol and finds it helps him with feeling more extroverted, daring, or happy, he will find drinking to be fun and appealing. This is a time of exploration, and his impulse control is not yet refined. This can result in binge drinking, as he may not yet know his limits with alcohol consumption, which can lead to additional risky behaviors including driving under the influence. Drinking in excess can lead to alcoholism or even alcohol poisoning in some cases.

THE EFFECTS OF ALCOHOL ON THE TEENAGE BRAIN

As discussed in earlier chapters, your son does not have full capacity of his frontal lobe as he journeys through adolescence into adulthood. Other parts of his brain are also developing, and the use of alcohol can affect his brain development. The limbic system, which is responsible for dealing with emotions, can be impacted by the use of alcohol. Furthermore, the fact that his brain is still developing makes him more susceptible and vulnerable to damaging effects on the brain, both short-term and long-term. The effects of drinking on the teenage brain can be irreversible in some instances. The younger a teen is when he starts consuming alcohol, the more likely he is to develop a serious problem or addiction later in life. The CDC notes that alcohol is the most common and misused drug among youth. One of the impacts that alcohol use and misuse has on teens is creating impairments in learning and memory retention.

Since your son's frontal lobe is still developing, alcohol consumption can negatively impact his executive functioning, including planning, organization, cognitive control, and decision-making. Alcohol can have a stronger effect on adolescent brains than adult brains and can significantly impair learning and memory. Drinking can also result in poor decision-making, such as drinking and driving, which can lead to fatal car accidents or serious bodily harm to your teen, his passengers, or others on the road.

Alcohol can slow down brain function, and this can cause issues with coordination, retaining new information, short-term memory, and emotion control. As for short-term effects on the brain, teens can experience blackouts, hangovers, or fuzzy memories and recollection of the previous night. Although these effects minimize as alcohol metabolizes and leaves the body, continued use of alcohol can result in long-term effects. Binge drinking and long-term alcohol use can turn into dependency, addiction, and other health problems.

Another part of the brain that can be impacted or suffer from cell destruction as a result of alcohol consumption is the hippocampus. This part of the brain is responsible for learning and memory. Long-term effects of extended use of alcohol in adolescence can include an underdeveloped hippocampus, which can impact the way your teen remembers new things and learns even well into his adulthood.

DEBUNKING THE RUMOR MILL:
I HEARD THAT SOME PARENTS LET KIDS HAVE PARTIES WITH ALCOHOL AS LONG AS THEY'RE HOME. SHOULD I BE DOING THAT?

In the United States, a person is not legally allowed to consume alcohol until the age of 21. Per the CDC, this was established in 1984 as a nationwide age, whereas prior to that it varied from state to state. Other countries have different ages ranging from 13 years of age in Burkina Faso (West Africa) to 25 in Eritrea (East Africa). There are also some countries, such as Afghanistan, that totally ban alcohol, so age is irrelevant.

The law in the United States prohibits the legal consumption of alcohol by a minor (under age 21) and establishments that knowingly serve alcohol to a minor run the risk of being fined and can even face jail time. By the same token, the expectation for parents is to abide by the same laws set forth for the public when it comes to underage drinking. Because the United States is a melting pot of cultures and ethnicities, these dynamics probably impact the choices you make in terms of allowing your child to consume alcohol before the legal drinking age. When you are in a different country that has a younger drinking age, it is up to your discretion whether or not you allow your son to drink legally, as they are allowed to do so with proof of identification.

Some parents believe that it is safer to allow their child (and sometimes their child's friends) to drink in their home so long as they are present. There are parents that generally believe this will allow their children to be exposed

continued >>

to alcohol in a setting that prevents them from drinking elsewhere and running the risk of driving while impaired. The fact of the matter is your son will likely drink in other settings away from you, so allowing him to drink in your home does not prevent that. Early consumption of alcohol has been shown to cause a higher likelihood of long-term effects regardless of the setting. Allowing your son to drink in your home will likely give him the impression you approve of his underage drinking. In short, allowing your son to drink in your home does not offer any benefits and can result in civil and criminal penalties for you, depending on your state of residence.

The Partnership for Drug-Free Kids and the Treatment Research Institute have created a website for parents that details legal liabilities based on their state of residence for serving alcohol to minors (socialhost.drugfree.org).

THE TRUTH (NOT D.A.R.E.) ABOUT DRUGS

Illicit drugs include marijuana, lysergic acid diethylamide (LSD), other hallucinogens, crack, cocaine, and heroin. Modern drug culture also includes the misuse of prescription drugs. Teens might have a misconception that prescribed drugs are less dangerous, but the misuse of prescription drugs can lead to short- and long-term effects and can even be deadly. Misuse occurs when a teen takes more than the recommended prescribed dose or when a teen takes medication that is not prescribed to him and without a doctor's supervision.

There are three main categories of prescription drugs that are currently being misused: 1) stimulants, such as Ritalin, commonly used to treat ADHD; 2) opiates, such as Vicodin, used to relieve pain; and 3) depressants, such as Xanax, used to treat anxiety or to promote sleep. In addition, it is important to note that social media, celebrities, and peers heavily influence modern teen drug culture. Celebrities and peers posting about risky behaviors that include drug use glamorize the use of drugs and make it seem more appealing to your teen. Studies show that teens who have social media accounts have a higher likelihood of engaging in drugs and alcohol use than those with no social media accounts or those who use social media less frequently.

Before talking to your teen about drug use, set boundaries, guidelines, and expectations you wish to convey to him, but also allow him to express his views on drugs. Some teens have a strong belief system that certain drugs are not harmful since they are natural and from the earth, such as marijuana coming from a plant. Although marijuana is now legal in some states, it is still illegal on the federal level and for minors to consume.

Due to marijuana becoming so mainstream, many teens view it as nonthreatening. Discuss what short- and long-term effects of engaging in the use of marijuana and other drugs—including the misuse of prescription drugs—can have on his brain. Include discussion about the decrease in inhibitions, which can lead him to engage in potentially dangerous and risky behaviors.

There are signs and behaviors your son may display that are indicative of a teen engaging in drug use. Some warning signs to take note of include the following: withdrawing socially, losing interest in family activities, being disrespectful toward family members or house rules, lying about activities, loss of valuable items or money, notable increases or decreases in appetite, engaging in abusive behavior, a decline in grades and school activity, becoming defiant and truant, losing interest in learning, sleeping in class, a sudden change in friendships, mood swings and erratic behavior, stealing, cheating, and a tendency to be argumentative.

If you suspect your son is using drugs or alcohol, take time to create a plan for yourself and approach him in a calm manner. Yelling and lecturing will create more walls and prevent this from being a productive conversation.

YES, YOU SHOULD BE
CONCERNED ABOUT VAPING

Vaping has become increasingly popular in recent years, and as of 2017, it has surpassed cigarette use among teens. The use of vape pens is on the rise and has more than doubled among adolescents from 2017 to 2019. Currently, teens and young adults comprise the highest percentage of the population that vapes. Men also have been found to be more likely to engage in vape use, which makes your son more susceptible to vaping.

Vaping is the use of an electronic cigarette, or e-cigarette, and contains liquid that is converted to vapor, which is then inhaled. Nicotine, marijuana, and hash oil are the most commonly used substances in vape pens. The increase in popularity of e-cigarettes among teens can be credited to marketing strategies geared toward teens and young adults. Teens also appreciate the low to no smell that comes from vaping, making it easier to hide from parents, teachers, coaches, and other authority figures.

The use of vape pens should be concerning for any parent of an adolescent. There are many dangers and risks associated with the use of vape pens. Nicotine is known to be highly addictive and harmful to the development of the adolescent brain. It can also lead to increased heart rate, blood pressure, and circulatory problems. The vapor that is produced by these pens can have harmful particles that can contribute to an increased risk for cancer. Vape use also irritates the lungs, and severe lung damage can be life-threatening.

If you are aware of your son using vape pens, it is vital that you contact a doctor if he displays any of the following symptoms: coughing, shortness of breath or chest pain, nausea, vomiting, diarrhea, fatigue, fever, or weight loss. The use of marijuana with vape pens has additional harmful and dangerous risks for your son, as excessive marijuana use had been specifically linked to an increased risk of psychosis in teens. When it comes to the use of marijuana, moderation matters.

DEBUNKING THE RUMOR MILL:
SHOULD I BE HONEST WITH MY TEEN ABOUT MY PAST RECREATIONAL DRUG USE?

Studies have found that admitting your past recreational drug use can be counterproductive. For some parents, sharing past drug use can be used as a learning tool based on, "Do as I say, not as I did." This does not prevent your child from experimenting and can even lead to him being more likely to want to try it for himself. Forums where this question is asked have mixed responses. Although some people talk about how learning about their parents' drug use benefited in keeping them from using drugs themselves, there are others who indicated it had the opposite effect.

Research has shown that the foundation of your relationship with your son is more important than the information you are sharing with him about your past use. The constructive messages you convey to him will have more of an impact on his drug use than your decision to share your past indiscretions.

What does this mean in terms of full disclosure? Although lying to your son is never encouraged, it is okay and even advised to be selective with the information you share and when you are sharing it with him. Some articles suggest outright denying drug use, but being selective and intentional with the information you share with your son has been proven to be the most successful in building trust, rapport, and communication. The information you choose to share should be on an as-needed basis and should be determined by your son's age. Be aware of the reasons you are choosing to share your history with your

continued >>

son and how it will benefit him. What is your ultimate goal with sharing your past with him? Are you trying to teach him through your past experiences and mistakes? Are you trying to prove that you were once cool, too? Ultimately, set clear and concise guidelines, rules and expectations to be followed in your home and use your best discretion when sharing your past with your son on this and other topics as well.

STUDY PREP: YOUR POSITIVE PARENTING NOTES

Five easy ways to incorporate positive parenting in your household as it relates to drug and alcohol use include the following:

1. Show interest/concern. Don't blame or shame. This is crucial to the dynamic of your relationship with your son. He does not want to feel micromanaged, lectured, or accused. This will only create a divide. Being overly judgmental and critical will be counterproductive to your relationship with your son. When having a conversation with him about sensitive topics, it is important to be factual and ask direct questions. Let him know why you are interested or concerned, and how you would like to support him. Remember to make it a conversation, not an argument or lecture. Conversations are give and take. Don't be the one that does all of the talking! This is a great time to engage in active listening.

2. Create a strong foundation of trust and communication. Communication is a key element for establishing solid trust with your son. If you are allowing open communication to flow, it will fortify your relationship with him. Trust

is important. The relationship he has with you and the way you create, build, and fortify trust will lead to healthy relationships into adulthood. Trust him to take on more responsibility as he gets older. As your child continues to mature in his independence continue to fortify your relationship and don't be afraid to allow him to continue in his growth toward autonomy. Be a support system and encourage his growth. Use open communication to lead your son to talk out and work through problems. Simply showing your son basic respect will increase his trust and strengthen your relationship foundation.

3. Parent actively and appropriately. Discuss the hard topics with your son early and on an ongoing basis, depending on his age and stage of development. Start having conversations about sex, drugs, alcohol, and vaping from an early age. Remember that the conversation that you have with your 12-year-old will vary from the conversation with your 17-year-old. At any age, allow for your son to have open and honest conversations about his views regarding tough topics and give him a voice. Talk through issues that arise instead of avoiding challenging subjects. Be open to having conversations about sensitive topics such as depression, anxiety, mental health, and risky behaviors.

4. Encourage good self-care. Have conversations about what self-care means and how you incorporate it in your daily life. Discuss the benefits of engaging in self-care, and support your son as he explores and implements self-care in his life. If you have commonalities, you can engage in self-care together such as walking around the neighborhood, attending a sports game, or meditating together. Create a schedule for your home and set bedtimes and meal routines. Self-care incorporates good hygiene, sleep, healthy eating, and exercise.

5. Parent by example. If you are asking your son to display responsibility, model the behavior that you want for him to engage in. What are the ways you teach him to make healthy and responsible decisions? Support him in learning effective coping strategies that will buoy his autonomy. As he continues to develop into adulthood, he learns from you and picks up on your healthy and unhealthy patterns of behavior. Show him affection, and spend quality time with him to demonstrate how important affection and quality time are. Demonstrate healthy expression of anger for your son. Normalize anger as well as other emotions for him in order to allow him to learn and grow in his willingness to express his feelings and emotions in an open and honest manner.

KEY TAKEAWAYS

In this chapter you have learned about the use, misuse, and abuse of alcohol and drugs, as well as the impact of alcohol on the teen brain and the pressures teens are faced with to engage in underage drinking. Identification of laws and possible consequences for adults who allow underage drinking were also explored. Drugs and their health and behavioral effects and consequences were also studied. We also discussed the appeal alcohol, drugs, and vaping have for your son. In addition, we delved into some of the short- and long-term effects and dangers any teen faces when engaging in alcohol or drug use.

- Teens and alcohol don't mix. Alcohol use and abuse can lead to harmful and long-term effects on your son's developing brain. Consumption of alcohol can lead to fuzziness in your son's perception, impacting his learning as well as short- and long-term memory. Alcohol use can also lower inhibitions, which leads to a higher likelihood of engaging in risky behaviors such as unsafe sex or driving under the influence.

- Teens and drugs don't mix. Although marijuana use is still popular among teens and young adults, prescription drug use is also on the rise. Opiates, depressants, and stimulants are some of the drugs teens use the most.

- Teens and vaping don't mix. Vaping has become more popular among teens than cigarette use. Vaping includes the use of nicotine and marijuana. Vaping is most appealing to teens due to marketing, social media posts, and the minimal to no smell that comes from the use of e-cigarettes.

- All of the above can affect your son's moods, behaviors, and functioning. Know the symptoms and warning signs that are indicative of drug or alcohol use. Have a non-accusatory conversation with your son to discuss the risks and dangers of drug and alcohol use. Get him help and be supportive of him quitting if he has issues with excessive use or addiction. Be aware of withdrawal symptoms and how you can support him in the event he attempts to withdraw from drugs or alcohol—professional medical attention is recommended.

GRADUATION & BEYOND

As you voyage alongside your son's adolescence, remember to implement the positive parenting techniques and tips provided throughout this book, with consistency and communication being key. Adolescence is indeed challenging, as your son is facing many societal pressures and stressors . . . with significant physiological changes on top of it all. Be aware of the unfolding of your child's developmental stages, acknowledging that he might not mature at the same pace as his peers or siblings—he could be a slow starter, or perhaps he is developing at breakneck speed. Yikes! Honor your son's individuality, and meet him where he is instead of rushing him through developmental stages or expecting his development to slow down.

Adolescence is tough on teens as they explore their interests and preferences in life while trying to fit in. They are going through puberty, developing autonomy, and figuring out who they are and who they want to be—that's a pretty full load. Be supportive of your son and his choices, but also set firm limits, boundaries, and expectations for him. Have clear and concise discussions about sex, love, drugs, alcohol, and other hard topics, but also make room for light conversations and small talk so your son doesn't feel family chat sessions are always pressure-filled. By establishing a routine of open communication on any topic, whether heavy or lighthearted, you give him permission to be up-front and honest with you.

Keep in mind that toxic masculinity impacts girls, boys, and parents. Identify any role it plays in your family dynamic, and pinpoint traits of it in your family that you wish to eradicate. Identify ways you perhaps engage in toxic masculinity or misogyny, and correct any missteps so you can teach your son to be more sensitive to such issues. You or other family members might have engaged in toxic masculinity without even realizing it based on cultural and familial dynamics. By taking accountability and speaking truthfully with your son, you break away from family norms to bust old mindless habits and begin new consciously healthier attitudes.

As he expresses himself, your son might present as moody and irritable. Recognize that he is experiencing not only physical changes but also emotional challenges as his brain continues to develop. Testosterone, too, plays a role in his development, impacting his growth sometimes before you can see physical evidence of it. During this time, he might withdraw from you and the family, as he is trying to figure out what the heck is happening to him. Honor his need for privacy and space, while making it clear that you are on his team and are there for support if he chooses to reach out to you.

The teenage brain is a complex one, not at full capacity until your son is in his mid-20s. During his development toward adulthood, he will learn from you as he explores how to engage in healthy decision-making. Due to the fact that his frontal lobe is still developing its connections, your son utilizes his hypothalamus for decision-making, which is why teens are prone to impulsive and risky behaviors. Although he is learning how to control his emotions and recognizing the repercussions of his impulsivity, it is important for you to set rules and expectations for him.

Peer pressure is a huge component for your son during adolescence. Risky behaviors teens commonly engage in include underage drinking, bullying, and defiance. If he engages in these types of behavior, have a conversation with him about it and establish consequences. Do what you say, and say what you mean! Hold him accountable for his actions, but rather than a prolonged punitive approach to your son's missteps, let these be opportunities for him to move on and apply what he has learned from the experiences—he'll likely make different choices in similar situations next time around.

This is a sensitive time for him, and some emotions might occur that create dysregulation for him. Be open with him about mental health, and if he needs professional help be supportive and encouraging about therapy. Therapy should not be presented as a punishment or seen as negative—break free of mental health stigmas.

Teenagers have their own forms of communication, and slang certainly comes into play. Note how slang has changed over time, and be up to date on his style of communication with his peers. Encourage and promote verbal expression of emotions and feelings.

Finally, please give yourself a pat on the back because parenting is not easy! Be kind to yourself as you go through ebbs and flows with your son. You are doing a great job—you're reading this book because you want to be the best parent you can be, right?—and you, too, are learning about your son and yourself as you go through the process. Be open to breaking unhealthy generational and cultural cycles, and remember that just because your son turns 18 and perhaps leaves home for college, the military, or employment, that doesn't mean you stop being a parent.

RESOURCES

The following resources are meant to provide additional support to your and/or your son:

SUICIDE PREVENTION

National Suicide Prevention Lifeline (suicidepreventionlifeline.org)

24/7 Hotline: 800-273-8255

The Trevor Project (www.thetrevorproject.org)

24/7 Hotline: 866-488-7386

Boys Town (www.boystown.org/Pages/default.aspx)

24/7 Hotline: 800-448-3000

Teen Line (www.teenline.org)

Hotline (6:00 p.m.–10:00 p.m.): 800-852-8336

TEEN RUNAWAYS

National Runaway Safeline (www.1800runaway.org)

Hotline: 800-RUNAWAY (800-786-2929)

Covenant House (www.covenanthouse.org)

BULLYING

PACER's National Bullying Prevention Center (www.pacer.org/bullying)

Center for the Prevention of Hate Violence
(www.preventinghate.org)

SOCIAL MEDIA

Organization for Social Media Safety (www.ofsms.org)

SEX EDUCATION

Sex Positive Families: 10 Best Sex Ed Resources for Families:
(sexpositivefamilies.com/10-best-sex-ed-resources-for-families)

Sex Ed for Social Change (SIECUS): Guidelines for Comprehensive Sexuality Education: (siecus.org/wp-content/uploads/2018
/07/Guidelines-CSE.pdf)

POSITIVE PARENTING

Centers for Disease Control and Prevention (CDC): Positive
Parenting Tips: (www.cdc.gov/ncbddd/childdevelopment
/positiveparenting/pdfs/teen-15-17-w-npa.pdf)

REFERENCES

"The 1 in 6 Statistic." 1in6. Accessed October 18, 2021. 1in6.org
/get-information/the-1-in-6-statistic.

"25 Interesting Facts About Hazing." Inside Hazing. Accessed October 18,
2021. www.insidehazing.com/statistics.

Abrams, Lindsay. "Study: Parents Are Better Off Not Admitting They've
Tried Drugs." *The Atlantic.* February 22, 2013. www.theatlantic.com
/health/archive/2013/02/study-parents-are-better-off-not
-admitting-theyve-tried-drugs/273384.

"Abstinence-Only Education States 2021." *World Population Review.*
Accessed October 18, 2021. worldpopulationreview.com/state
-rankings/abstinence-only-education-states.

"Abstinence-Only-Until-Marriage Programs." Planned Parenthood.
Accessed October 18, 2021. www.plannedparenthoodaction.org
/issues/sex-education/abstinence-only-programs.

"Age 21 Minimum Legal Drinking Age." Centers for Disease Control and
Prevention. Accessed October 26, 2021. www.cdc.gov/alcohol/fact
-sheets/minimum-legal-drinking-age.htm.

"Aggression." Merriam-Webster. Accessed September 14, 2021.
www.merriam-webster.com/dictionary/aggression.

Archer, John, Nicola Graham-Kevan, and Michelle Davies. "Testosterone and Aggression: A Reanalysis of Book, Starzyk, and Quinsey's
(2001) Study." *Aggression and Violent Behavior* 10, no. 2 (May 2004):
241–261. doi.org/10.1016/j.avb.2004.01.001.

Bagwell, Catherine L., and Michelle E. Schmidt. *Friendships in Childhood
and Adolescence.* New York: The Guilford Press, 2011.

Bahns, Angela J. "Preference, Opportunity, and Choice: A multilevel ana-
lysis of diverse friendship formation." *Group Processes & Intergroup
Relations* 22, no. 2 (February 2019): 233–52. doi.org/10.1177
/1368430217725390.

Blume, Howard. "RIOT AFTERMATH: Schools Cope With Impact of Riots
on Youth : Effects: Most students are confused by the unrest. Many

denounce the violence, but know someone who took part in looting."
Los Angeles Times. May 14, 1992.

Bostic, Jeff Q., Lisa Thurau, Mona Potter, and Stacy S. Drury. "Policing the
Teen Brain." *Journal of the American Academy of Child & Adolescent
Psychiatry* 53, no. 2 (February 2014): 127-129. doi.org/10.1016/j.jaac
.2013.09.021.

"Brain Map Frontal Lobes." Queensland Government. Accessed
September 14, 2021. www.health.qld.gov.au/abios/asp/bfrontal.

Brown, Catherine. "Male Body Image Issues—Body Image Affects Boys,
Too." *Your Teen Magazine*. Accessed October 18, 2021. yourteenmag
.com/health/teenager-mental-health/male-body-image-issues.

Burch, Kelly. "How social media affects the mental health of teenagers."
Insider. March 16, 2020. www.insider.com/how-does-social-media
-affect-teenagers.

Carman, Aaron J., Rennie Ferguson, Robert Cantu, R. Dawn Comstock,
Penny A. Dacks, Steven T. DeKosky, Sam Gandy, et al. "Mind the
gaps—advancing research into short-term and long-term neuropsy-
chological outcomes of youth sports-related concussions." *Nature
Reviews Neurology* 11, no. 4 (April 2015): 230–244. doi.org/10.1038
/nrneurol.2015.30.

"Children in Progressive-Era America." Digital Public Library of America.
Accessed September 14, 2021. dp.la/exhibitions/children
-progressive-era/childhood-postwar-america/teenage-culture.

Clark, Christina. *Boys, Girls and Communication: Their Views, Confidence
and Why These Skills Matter*. London: National Literacy Trust, 2011.

Collins, W. Andrew, Deborah P. Welsh, and Wyndol Furman. "Adolescent
romantic relationships." *Annual Review of Psychology* 60
(January 2009): 631–652. doi.org/10.1146/annurev.psych.60.110707
.163459.

Denson, Nida, and Mitchell J. Chang. "Racial Diversity Matters: The
Impact of Diversity-Related Student Engagement and Institutional

Context." *American Educational Research Journal* 46, no. 2 (June 2009): 322–53. doi.org/10.3102/0002831208323278.

DeWitt, Douglas M., and Lori J. DeWitt. "A Case of High School Hazing: Applying Restorative Justice to Promote Organizational Learning." *NASSP Bulletin* 96, no. 3 (August 2012): 228–242. doi.org/10.1177 /0192636512452338.

Dorman, Gayle. *Living with 10- to 15-Year-Olds: A Parent Education Curriculum.* Chapel Hill: University of North Carolina Press, 1992.

Dunne, Brigit. "The Importance of Positively Talking to Your Kids About Sex." Zacharias Sexual Abuse Center. May 13, 2021. zcenter.org /blog/the-importance-of-positively-talking-to-your-kids-about-sex.

Enan, Robin. "The Newest Teen Slang Trends of 2021." *FamilyEducation.* Last modified October 12, 2021. www.familyeducation.com/teens /a-parents-guide-to-the-latest-teen-slang.

"Everything You Wanted to Know About Puberty." Nemours KidsHealth. Accessed September 14, 2021. https://kidshealth.org/en/teens /puberty.html.

Garey, Juliann. "Marijuana and Psychosis." Child Mind Institute. Accessed October 26, 2021. childmind.org/article/marijuana-and-psychosis.

"Glossary of Terms." Human Rights Campaign. Accessed October 26, 2021. www.hrc.org/resources/glossary-of-terms.

Goodman, Brenda. "Concussions Might Affect Kids and Adults Differently." WebMD. November 29, 2011. www.webmd.com/children /news/20111129/concussions-might-affect-kids-adults-differently#1.

Greitemeyer, Tobias. "Effects of Prosocial Media on Social Behavior: When and Why Does Media Exposure Affect Helping and Aggression?" *Current Directions in Psychological Science* 20, no. 4 (August 2011): 251–255. doi.org/10.1177/0963721411415229.

"The Guidelines for Comprehensive Sexuality Education." Sexuality Information and Education Council of the United States. Accessed October 18, 2021. siecus.org/resources/the-guidelines.

"Hazing: Not Just a College Problem Anymore." *Education World.* Last modified November 4, 2011. www.educationworld.com/a_issues /issues123.shtml.

"Hazing: The Issue." StopHazing Research Lab. December, 2020. stophazing.org/issue.

Heilman, B., C. M. Guerrero-López, C. Ragonese, M. Kelberg, and G. Barker. *The Cost of the Man Box: A Study on the Economic Impacts of Harmful Masculine Stereotypes in the United States.* Washington and London: Promundo-US and Unilever, 2019.

Herbert, Joe. *Testosterone: Sex, Power, and the Will to Win.* New York: Oxford University Press, 2015.

Hilliard, Jena. "The Influence Of Social Media On Teen Drug Use." Addiction Center. July 16, 2019. www.addictioncenter.com/community/social-media-teen-drug-use.

Hirsch, Irvin H. "Puberty in Boys." Merck Manual. Last modified March 2021. www.merckmanuals.com/home/men-s-health-issues/biology-of-the-male-reproductive-system/puberty-in-boys.

Howard, Jacqueline. "The Countries Where Drinking Is Banned until 25—Or Allowed at 13." CNN Health. January 1, 2019. www.cnn.com/2018/12/31/health/legal-drinking-age-world-explainer-parenting-intl/index.html.

Institute of Medicine and National Research Council. *Adolescent Development and the Biology of Puberty: Summary of a Workshop on New Research.* Washington: The National Academies Press, 1999.

Li, Pamela. "Positive Parenting—The Definitive Guide And 9 Essential Tips." *Parenting For Brain.* Last modified August 6, 2021. www.parentingforbrain.com/what-is-positive-parenting.

Li, Pamela. "4 Types of Parenting Styles and Their Effects On The Child." *Parenting For Brain.* Last modified November 25, 2021. www.parentingforbrain.com/4-baumrind-parenting-styles.

Morin, Amy. "What Is Toxic Masculinity?" *Verywell Mind.* Last modified November 25, 2020. www.verywellmind.com/what-is-toxic-masculinity-5075107#what-is-toxic-masculinity.

"Myths Debunked: Underage Drinking of Alcohol at Home Leads to Real Consequences for Both Parents and Teens." Partnership to End Addiction. May 22, 2013. drugfree.org/newsroom/news-item/myths-debunked-underage-drinking-of-alcohol-at-home-leads-to-real-consequences-for-both-parents-and-teens.

Nieschlag, Eberhard, Hermann M. Behre, and Susan Nieschlag, eds. *Testosterone: Action, Deficiency, Substitution*, 4th ed. New York: Cambridge University Press, 2012.

"Over Half of U.S. Teens Have Had Sexual Intercourse by Age 18." Centers for Disease Control and Prevention. June 22, 2017. www.cdc.gov /nchs/pressroom/nchs_press_releases/2017/201706_NSFG.htm.

Reidy, Dennis E., Joanne P. Smith-Darden, Kai S. Cortina, Roger M. Kernsmith, and Poco D. Kernsmith. "Masculine Discrepancy Stress, Teen Dating Violence, and Sexual Violence Perpetration Among Adolescent Boys." *Journal of Adolescent Health* 56, no. 6 (June 2015): 619–624. doi.org/10.1016/j.jadohealth.2015.02.009.

"Relationships and romance: pre-teens and teenagers." Raising Children Network. Accessed October 4, 2021. raisingchildren.net.au/pre-teens /communicating-relationships/romantic-relationships/teen -relationships.

Schaeffer, Katherine. "Before recent outbreak, vaping was on the rise in U.S., especially among young people." Pew Research Center. September 26, 2019. www.pewresearch.org/fact-tank/2019/09/26 /vaping-survey-data-roundup.

Schubert, Kristin. "Building a Culture of Health: Promoting Healthy Relationships and Reducing Teen Dating Violence." *Journal of Adolescent Health* 56, no. 2 (February 2015): S3–S4. doi.org/10.1016/j.jadohealth .2014.11.015.

"Serious Mental Health Challenges among Older Adolescents and Young Adults." SAMHSA. May 6, 2014. www.samhsa.gov/data/sites/default /files/sr173-mh-challenges-young-adults-2014/sr173-mh-challenges -young-adults-2014/sr173-mh-challenges-young-adults-2014.htm.

Sifferlin, Alexandra. "Why Teenage Brains Are So Hard to Understand." *Time*. September 8, 2017. time.com/4929170/inside-teen-teenage -brain.

Silver, Sharon. "Does Roughhousing Lead to Violence?" *Proactive Parenting*. May 22, 2015. proactiveparenting.net/does-roughhousing-lead -to-violence.

Spurr, Cameron, and Emily Forgash. "Confronting Toxic Masculinity." *The Standard*. March 5, 2021. standard.asl.org/16764/features /confronting-toxic-masculinity.

Steiner, Andy. "What should parents tell kids about past drug or alcohol use?" *MinnPost*. October 30, 2017. www.minnpost.com/mental-health-addiction/2017/10/what-should-parents-tell-kids-about-past-drug-or-alcohol-use.

Stewart, Joanna, Sandra Garrido, Cherry Hense, and Katrina McFerran. "Music Use for Mood Regulation: Self-Awareness and Conscious Listening Choices in Young People with Tendencies to Depression." *Frontiers in Psychology* 10 (May 2019): 1199–1199. doi.org/10.3389/fpsyg.2019.01199.

Stowers, C. "The Hurried Child." *New Internationalist* 343 (March 2002): 22. newint.org/features/2002/03/05/hurried.

"Strength Training." *Nemours KidsHealth*. August, 2018. kidshealth.org/en/teens/strength-training.html.

"Teenagers & Sexual Violence Infographic." National Sexual Violence Research Center. February, 2019. www.nsvrc.org/teenagers-sexual-violence-infographic.

Ucciferri, Frannie. "Parents' Ultimate Guide to Discord." *Common Sense Media*. Last modified March 1, 2020. www.commonsensemedia.org/blog/parents-ultimate-guide-to-discord.

"Underage Drinking." Centers for Disease Control and Prevention. Accessed October 26, 2021. www.cdc.gov/alcohol/fact-sheets/underage-drinking.htm.

"Underage Drinking in the Home." Partnership to End Addiction. Accessed October 26, 2021. socialhost.drugfree.org.

"Vaping: What You Need to Know." *Nemours KidsHealth*. Accessed October 26, 2021. kidshealth.org/en/parents/e-cigarettes.html.

Vargas, Robert. "Being in 'Bad' Company: Power Dependence and Status in Adolescent Susceptibility to Peer Influence." *Social Psychology Quarterly* 74, no. 3 (August 2011): 310–332. doi.org/10.1177/0190272511414546.

Vente, Teresa, Mary Daley, Elizabeth Killmeyer, and Laura K. Grubb. "Association of Social Media Use and High-Risk Behaviors in Adolescents: Cross-Sectional Study." *JMIR Pediatrics and Parenting* 3, no. 1 (May 2020): e18043. doi.org/10.2196/18043.

Weaver, Rheyanne. "The Link Between Clothing Choices and Emotional States." *GoodTherapy*. March 30, 2012. www.goodtherapy.org/blog /link-between-clothing-choices-and-emotional-states-0330124.

"What Is a Concussion?" Centers for Disease Control and Prevention. Accessed October 18, 2021. www.cdc.gov/headsup/basics /concussion_whatis.html.

"What Is Bullying." *StopBullying.gov*. Accessed October 18, 2021. www.stopbullying.gov/bullying/what-is-bullying.

"What Is Trauma?" Integrated Listening Systems. Accessed September 14, 2021. integratedlistening.com/what-is-trauma.

"What should I teach my high school–aged teen about sex and sexuality?" Planned Parenthood. Accessed October 18, 2021. www .plannedparenthood.org/learn/parents/high-school/what-should -i-teach-my-high-school-aged-teen-about-sex-and-sexua.

Whittle, Sarah, Julian G. Simmons, Meg Dennison, Nandita Vijayakumar, Oril Schwartz, Marie B. H. Yap, Lisa Sheeber, and Nicholas B. Allen. "Positive parenting predicts the development of adolescent brain structure: a longitudinal study." *Developmental Cognitive Neuroscience* 8 (April 2014): 7–17. doi.org/10.1016/j.dcn.2013.10.006.

INDEX

A

Aggression, 20–21, 61
Alcohol use, 40, 103, 104–108, 114
Amygdala, 22, 40
Anti-femininity, 9
Authoritative parenting, ix–x
Autonomy, 69, 83, 89, 91

B

Belonging, desire for, 3–4
Body image, 59–60, 64–66, 70–71
Bonding, 69
Boundaries, 13, 55, 57, 76, 86
"Boys will be boys" excuse, 6–8. *See also*
    Toxic masculinity
Brain
    development of, 22–24, 28–29, 118
    effects of alcohol on, 105–106, 114
Breaks from each other, taking, 28
Bullying, 57, 59, 61–62, 71. *See also*
    Cyberbullying; Hazing

C

Communication. *See also* Conversations
    about feelings and emotions, 33–34, 43
    methods of, 32–33
    open, 7–8, 84, 112–113
    styles, 119
Concussions, 67–68
Consent, 51, 73, 75–76, 86
Consequences, 11, 13, 24, 41
Conversations
    about dating, 50–51
    about feelings and emotions, 99
    about parental drug use, 111–112
    about relationships, 52–53, 57
    about self-expression, 99–100
    about sex, 45, 51, 73–75, 77–78, 83–85

about toxic masculinity, 9
open- vs. close-ended
    questions, 13, 35–36, 43
physical activity during, 33
tips, x–xi
Criticism, 42
Cyberbullying, 40

D

Dating, 50–54
Death metal, 97–98
Decision-making skills, 24
Diversity, 47–48, 70
Drug use, 103–104, 108–109, 115

E

Eating disorders, 59, 65
Emotion coaching, xi–xii
Enthusiastic consent, 73, 75–76, 86
Erikson's stages of psychosocial
    development, 34
Ethnicity, defined, 47
Expectations, 11, 13, 24, 26–27,
    41, 55, 57, 69–70, 84–85

F

Family meetings, 56
Feelings and emotions
    communicating about, 33–34, 43
    conversations about, 99
"Flight, fight, freeze, or fawn"
    response, 22–23, 29
Friendships
    "bad influences," 49–50
    diversity in, 47–48
    healthy, 52–53
    importance of strong, 46–47, 55
Frontal lobe, 23–24, 26, 29, 105–106

ACKNOWLEDGMENTS

To my parents: thank you for the sacrifices you made to create an environment where your children could thrive and succeed, by immigrating to this country with the hope of providing more for your family.

To my mother: Although you are no longer physically with us, I know you watch over me with pride. Thank you for teaching me to be tenacious, speak my mind, and to always strive for more.

Thank you to the man who loved me through the times I didn't know how to love myself.

Thank you to the little hands and feet that brought light back into my life after major loss.

ABOUT THE AUTHOR

 **MARISSA GARCIA SORIA, MSW, LCSW,** is a first-generation Mexican-American born and raised in Los Angeles, where she has worked with teens and their families for 20 years. Marissa is passionate about her work with youth and their families as they navigate through cultural and familial dynamics in order to break intergenerational and familial toxic cycles. Marissa owns a group practice in Southern California that aims to provide a welcoming and all-encompassing approach to the community, including LGBTQIA+ and POC with a focus on the Latinx and Spanish-speaking community. Marissa strives to provide a safe and welcoming space for clients and their family members to allow for them explore and embrace their true, authentic selves. During her spare time, she enjoys spending time with her family, friends, and pets, as well as traveling and hiking.